Contents

It seems like there are a million books out there that promise to help you get a job.

This book is different.

Lots of people will tell you what they think job interviewers are looking for.

We ***know*** what interviewers are looking for.

At Development Dimensions International (DDI), we're in the business of teaching managers how to interview job candidates. We work with organizations that want to do a better job of selecting the right people. For almost 30 years, we've been training managers in a process we call Targeted Selection®. The Targeted Selection method is a simple one. It's based on the idea that a person's past behavior predicts future performance.

Think about some of the questions you've been asked in job interviews. Does "What's your best quality?" sound familiar? How would you answer that question? You'd probably say something general such as, "I'm a hard worker," or "I'm a quick learner." And don't forget that old favorite, "I'm a people person." When you give answers like that, what does an interviewer learn about you? What have you said to demonstrate the benefits of hiring you over any of the other people who want the job?

What does being a "people person" actually mean, anyway? If you're good with people, that might mean you have a knack for convincing people to do things. It might also mean that you show a lot of concern for other people's needs. Or it might mean that you work well in groups or teams. It might mean all those things.

Your past behavior is a specific time when you led a meeting or made a personnel decision or coached a team. When you talk about your behavior, you're not discussing what you think or how you feel. Your behavior is what you've actually done. We call an example of a past behavior a STAR because a complete example includes a ***situation*** or a ***task***, the specific ***action*** you took, and the ***result*** of your action.

After hearing such specific information about your past behavior, an interviewer can draw a conclusion about your future performance—and make an accurate evaluation of how you'll perform in the job you want.

Targeted Selection training sessions give our clients the tools to do just that. We've worked with more than 7,000 organizations to help their managers make accurate and consistent decisions about whom to hire and promote. Our clients include McDonald's, JCPenney, Citicorp, Motorola, Toyota, General Motors, Avis, Kraft Foods, Eli Lilly, and Coca-Cola. In the past year nearly one million interviewers were trained in the Targeted Selection system.

Our consultants spend time with these clients and perform a job analysis, which consists of talking to managers and employees, asking questions, and getting to the heart of what they're looking for in a colleague. We find out what kind of performance they expect for each position being analyzed. We then classify these expectations into dimensions of performance. Dimensions are specific types of behaviors, such as leadership or planning and organizing.

We help managers develop interview questions that seek information about candidates' past behaviors—STAR examples in specific dimensions. After the interviews the managers use the information to determine which candidate is best suited to their needs.

Our system enables organizations to ensure that applicants are considered fairly: All candidates for a particular job are judged on the same job-related criteria. This system eliminates worries about discrimination or bias. And managers can be sure that they're hiring the very best people.

DDI is recognized as a world leader in interviewer training and employee selection. In fact, it was while President and CEO Dr. William C. Byham was delivering a keynote address to a human resources conference that we were asked to consider sharing our expert knowledge on interviewing with the people on the other side of the desk—the job seekers. That's how the idea for this book was conceived.

We began by thinking about the kinds of information that would be most helpful to people going on job interviews. Plenty of books on the market offer advice on things like what to wear, but not much practical advice on how to answer interview questions. So we designed *Landing the Job You Want* to help you:

- Know what to expect from an interview.
- Prepare for the interview.
- Handle a difficult interviewer.
- Critique your interview performance in order to do better the next time.
- Decide whether a job is right for you.

If you're reading this book, odds are you've got some important things on your mind. Maybe you've just been told that your job is being eliminated—or that it might be. Perhaps you've heard a rumor that your company is being reorganized or sold and that everyone will have to bid for a job in the new organization. Maybe today something snapped, and you realized that you just can't keep doing the same job forever.

Whatever your situation—finding a place for yourself in a changing organization, leaving your present job, returning to the workforce after an absence, or finishing school and looking for your first professional job—you're probably feeling confused and anxious.

Does it seem as if everyone you know is offering you advice? And are they all contradicting one another? Our goal is to offer you practical advice and useful tools for interview preparation, but we also want the book to be enjoyable and easy to read, so we created four characters to illustrate some important aspects of interviewing skills. Though fictional, their stories are based on the real-life experiences of job seekers in today's market.

In chapter 1, you'll meet Sara, Tom, Amanda, and Derek. They're four average people who happen to stop by the same coffee shop. They also happen to be on their way to or from job interviews. In the chapters that follow, you'll learn more about the challenges they encounter and what they learn.

- **Sara** is looking for a job in public relations. Although she has excellent writing and communication skills, she is having trouble breaking into the field she's chosen. She is interviewing with an international PR agency for an entry-level position.
- **Tom** is a production manager for one of his company's largest plants. The corporation's new strategy has created a leadership

position in the project management group at corporate headquarters. Tom wants that job, which would mean a significant promotion.

- **Amanda** has been raising her children full-time, but has decided to pursue a career outside the home. Her strong performance in design classes and her interest in fashion led her to seek a buyer's position in the women's apparel division of a large department store.

- **Derek** is an engineer and developer for a large defense contractor that is starting a new division to make products for the private sector. Derek wants to participate in this venture, and after 10 years as an engineer, he seeks to apply his technical knowledge in a different way by working with the new division's marketing department.

Our characters' adventures during their interviews highlight in an entertaining way common problems, misconceptions, or mistakes encountered by job seekers. Preparing for a job interview can be a demanding task, so we want to add as much enjoyment as possible to the experience.

Because you probably feel bombarded with job-hunting tips and information, we deliver our concepts through brief instructional sections filled with examples and language that's easily understood. We supplement those sections with exercises in which you have a chance to apply the concepts. These exercises help you prepare for all your interviews throughout your job search. They give you a framework for organizing your experiences into specific behaviors, which you can compare with the job's requirements to decide if you are qualified for and suited to the job you are seeking. And because completing these exercises will give you a clearer picture of the job, you can make an educated guess about the questions your interviewer will ask and prepare answers for those questions.

The best way to use this book is to read it from cover to cover and fill in the exercises as you go. We believe that this approach will most effectively develop your interviewing skills. And once you've completed the book, you'll have a valuable reference that will include our interviewing techniques as well as your own strategies.

We've got a few shortcuts to offer, though, in case you don't have the time to work through the entire book right now.

If your interview is tomorrow:
Read chapters 2 through 7 (pages 11-116), completing the exercises as you go. You'll practice giving information about yourself (past

behavior in the form of STAR examples) that will help your interviewer predict your future performance. You'll also identify the most important information to discuss in your interview. This information is classified into three categories of dimensions: what you know, how you apply what you know, and what motivates you. And get a good night's sleep!

If you're on a bus, train, or plane on your way to an interview:
Read chapter 2 (pages 11-28), skim chapters 3 through 6 (pages 29-98), and then read chapter 7 (pages 99-116). Look over the preparation exercises in each chapter and complete them if you have time. You'll learn about the most effective way to discuss your experience and identify the three general categories of information (dimensions) to discuss in your interview: what you know, how you apply what you know, and what motivates you.

If you're gulping down lunch and your interview is later this afternoon:
Skim chapters 2 through 5 (pages 11-86) and review the preparation exercise in chapter 2. You'll have a general format for how to phrase your answers so that you give your interviewer the most valuable information possible.

If you're sitting in the lobby waiting for your interviewer to come out and shake your hand:
Review chapter 2 (pages 11-28). This will keep the "past behavior predicts future performance" model and STAR format fresh in your mind. And take a deep breath!

Once you have read this book, the preparation exercises and appendixes will be useful tools for preparing for all the interviews throughout your job search. Appendix D discusses how you can apply the material in this book to your long-term career planning.

Introductory Exercise

The Job You Want

Describe the job you'd like to have.

Write down the most important tasks you'd perform on a regular basis in that job.

If you're not sure what job you'd like to have, write down the things that you would most like to do in a day (or week) at work.

We'll return to what you wrote here as we move through the other exercises. Feel free to change or elaborate on your comments as you think of new possibilities.

A CLEAN, WELL-LIT ESTABLISHMENT: THEY COULD HAVE CALLED IT THE NEED-A-JOB CAFE

1

College Grad Looks for First Job

Production Manager Seeks Promotion

At-Home Mom Tries for New Career

Engineer Hopes to Switch to Marketing

1

A CLEAN, WELL-LIT ESTABLISHMENT: THEY COULD HAVE CALLED IT THE NEED-A-JOB CAFE

The Hav-a-Java Cafe was one of those gourmet coffee places that had been popping up around the city. Some people claimed to hate them and said that they weren't real coffeehouses or, at least, not the ones they remembered. But many of those same people stopped at the Hav-a-Java Cafe every morning on the way to work. It was right next to the train station. Ed, the guy who worked behind the counter, knew the train schedules; he could predict when lines would form and when a lull would occur. In the mornings no one ever sat at the tables. And no one ever ordered decaf.

The afternoons were different. Ed made a point of getting to know the people who occupied his tables then. They were an interesting bunch, and from time to time Ed thought about collecting their stories. An aspiring filmmaker (read film school dropout), Ed often imagined how he'd capture the quiet desperation of his afternoon patrons. ✯

College Grad Looks for First Job

Sara Tecktip stopped in just before lunchtime and ordered a decaf hazelnut and a buttered roll. She had a young face—she could have been 16—but she was wearing a business suit and carrying a briefcase. Sara drank only half her coffee and ate a few bites of her roll. The grimace she wore when she paid the check made Ed think she was probably broke. He thought about wrapping up the rest of the roll for her or telling her to keep the tip, but decided against it. Everybody has pride.

Sara checked her lipstick three times in the pocket mirror she had pulled from her briefcase. She was glad she remembered to bring the mirror. This morning she had packed the case with her good shoes, makeup, two hairbrushes, hair spray, an umbrella, an extra pair of stockings, a map, a magazine and a paperback novel, her headphones and four tapes (including one for meditation), sunglasses, a sewing kit (in case she lost a button), dental floss, and gum. Her attaché's agreeable bulge made her look busy and important. In the back pocket of the case, she had slipped a folder containing 10 copies of her resume, plus writing samples and 10 copies of her transcript, which said "VOID" across them because, as it turned out, they weren't supposed to be photocopied.

The cafe was next door to Thompson Towers, the office building where Sara was going to meet Ingrid Zwerner, founder of Zwerner International Public Relations. Sara slipped off her sneakers and slid her feet into the navy pumps she had bought especially for today.

It was a clear day, and Sara took the bright sunshine as a good omen. Lately she'd been feeling desperate. Her parents, who had been so supportive of her taking the time to find the right job, were starting to get edgy. Last night when Sara was getting a pep talk from her college roommate, her mother had muttered, "I don't think I'd be making long-distance calls if I

didn't have a job." Were they tired of having her back at home? It didn't matter, she told herself; she had been smart to wait. Her friends who had taken the first jobs that came along were all miserable. She was certain that this job at ZIPR was going to work out for her, and she'd be moving out of her parents' house soon.

Maybe comparative literature was a useless major, as her parents always claimed. Maybe she should have studied accounting—even though she hated it. Sara was determined to prove her parents wrong, and yet terrified that they had been right.

She finally took a deep breath. In a few minutes she'd walk out of the cafe and into the office building. She'd talk with Ms. Zwerner. She'd go home. Tonight she'd meet her friend Dan for ice cream; maybe they'd see a movie. There was no reason to panic.

During her four years at college, Sara had studied hard. When she wasn't studying, she was working as a waitress. And when she wasn't working, she was at the university's newspaper office, writing her column. It seemed as if there should have been some reward for all that effort—she should have been the one who had to decide among three fabulous job offers. But, somehow, she hadn't managed to find a job. At graduation when people were asking one another, "What are you doing next year?" she would shrug and say that she was going to work on her writing.

August came and went. The lease on her apartment was up. Her savings were almost gone, and she still had no job. Not even any prospects. The 200 resumes she'd sent out yielded an impressive collection of rejection letters from all over the country, which, for lack of anything more productive to do, she had filed alphabetically. She had swallowed her pride and moved back home.

Sara took one last sip of coffee and walked toward Thompson Towers. She checked her reflection in the revolving door and went inside. On the fifteenth floor she found herself staring at the polished brass letters that proclaimed "Zwerner International Public Relations" and imagined herself seeing them every day as she walked into her own office. This just had to work out. It had to.

Production Manager Seeks Promotion

Tom DeSandro had just missed the 4:10, and there wasn't another train until 4:50. He took an iced tea from the cooler, slammed it on the counter, and paid for it without another word. He ignored the straw and napkin the man behind the counter offered and opened the bottle, closing his eyes and cocking his head back to take a long drink.

The way Tom figured it, he had a right to be angry. He had started working for the General Equipment Company almost 25 years ago, just after high school graduation. He liked his job and the people he worked with. With a house and two cars, he was doing better than a lot of other guys he knew. Of course, JoAnne's salary helped, but he knew he was a good provider. The girls, 9 and 17, were great kids, healthy and doing well in school. He knew he'd been lucky, but he wanted more. He wanted to be a success.

He was tired of wondering if they were going to cut production at the plant and if he'd lose his job. And JoAnne never knew what to expect with her schedule. Lately the hospital seemed to give fewer hours to the nurses and more to the assistants, who worked for less money.

This job would be a big promotion—and a big change. He would move from the plant to Corporate. And he'd be responsible for more than managing the production of components—he'd coordinate all the major projects at GenEquip. The senior executives were excited about this idea—the leader of the project management team would report directly to them. Tom had a hard time picturing himself in a meeting with those guys. He'd talked to them before, of course, and they knew him from the work that he'd done on the TQM project a few years ago.

Tom's friend Joe said that the success of that effort convinced the senior executives to establish a centralized project management function. Joe had convinced Tom to apply for the position when it was posted. At first, Tom didn't even tell JoAnne about it. He figured he'd never make it

past the first round, an interview with Robin in Human Resources. He'd known Robin for years—they'd started with the company within a couple of weeks of each other and gone through orientation together. As it turned out, the interview with Robin went great. The second round was a day of tests and simulations, which he was sure he'd blown, but he made it through that too. Two weeks ago when he found out he'd made it to the interview round, he had finally told JoAnne.

It was like the time a few years ago when he'd decided to go back to school. JoAnne, convinced that he was having an affair, had been ready to leave him when he broke down and told her what he was really doing at night. He couldn't stand to have her see him fail, so he didn't want to tell her about the class until it was done. When he finally told her about this job, he felt a lot more confident. It seemed like it was meant to be. Joe almost had him convinced he had a lock on it. And JoAnne, sensing his confidence, had beamed when he told her about it. She had even called her brother.

Today, though, practically everything had gone wrong for Tom. He had been tied up at the plant and barely got to the city on time. In the lobby of the corporate office, he'd met that kid—the guy could not have been more than 25—who said he also had an interview. That had set Tom off. Some MBA whose hands had never even gotten dirty was completely wrong for the job. But that was what they would want; he was sure of it. By the time the elevator stopped on the eleventh floor, he was convinced that his job already belonged to the other candidate.

Despite that thought, Tom wasn't ready to give up. He shook his interviewer's hand with extra firmness and, on the way to the meeting room, rehearsed how he would describe all the things he had done for GenEquip, all his hard work. Tom wanted to come right out and say it: He deserved the job. But he knew saying it wouldn't do him any good. He had to prove it.

Afterward, he was sure the interview had been a disaster.

And then he'd missed the train.

As he threw open the cafe's front door, he nearly knocked over a woman with bright blue eyes.

At-Home Mom Tries for New Career

The first thing people noticed about Amanda Bodnar was her eyes—a shade of blue that few people have, but everyone recognizes. Bright eyes, not exactly smiling, but paying attention to whoever comes into view. Amanda didn't look away when she gave Ed her order or when she pulled the black organizer from the matching briefcase.

Amanda thought she looked serene, but her stomach was churning with anxiety. This was the first job interview she'd gone on since making her "declaration." Her friends had all said she'd have to go through dozens of interviews and that she should consider the first few as practice. But she had a feeling about this one.

Then again, maybe it was indigestion. She sipped her peppermint tea—someone had told her that peppermint is supposed to calm nerves—and thought about what she would tell Jim. Would she say the interview had gone well? She thought it had, but then what if she didn't get the job? It would just make her seem all the more naive—clueless, as her son would say. But what would happen if she acted as if it had gone badly, and then she got it?

It was an odd hour. No working person would have a break at this time, and anyone heading home this early would go directly to the station. It was nice, though, this place. Quiet. Peaceful. She was almost able to relax here, to lose herself in thought. It was something she couldn't do easily at home.

Amanda wasn't sure if taking a job was the right thing to do, but she knew she had to try it. She wanted to spend her days with adults, to have people think of her not as Jim's wife or Liz and Brendan's mother, but as Amanda. Herself. Brendan, her youngest, was practically a teenager. And Liz was in her second year of college. Amanda was afraid that if she didn't go back to work now, she'd never do it. The kids would be away at college and starting their own lives, and there she'd be—learning to knit or something. Most of the women she knew held full-time

jobs even when their children were a lot younger than hers. Of course, those women didn't have husbands with jobs like Jim's.

She was proud of her marriage and proud of her husband and family. It wasn't that she felt she needed a job to add meaning to her life, but she did feel something was missing. Jim couldn't understand it. He asked her how she could think of taking a job, with him just being promoted to detective sergeant. He was going to be working crazy hours, covering all the shifts that the senior officers didn't want. Jim said he needed her at home. It wasn't that he objected to her working—they could always use the money—but the timing was wrong.

Although Amanda understood her husband's point of view, she had a sense of urgency about finding a job. She couldn't explain it, but she felt compelled to act on it. It wasn't like she was going back to being a flight attendant. She wasn't going to be traveling.

The cup of tea had relaxed her. Amanda decided to try to take things as they came. If this job didn't work out, something else would. Jim would come around and see how much having a job meant to her.

As Amanda pulled on her coat, she thought about how much she'd enjoy being a fashion buyer for Willowbee's. The art courses she'd taken over the years had sharpened her sense of aesthetics, and she had an eye for good design. "Maybe I'll really get the job," she thought, as she left the cafe and smiled a timid smile.

Engineer Hopes to Switch to Marketing

Derek Robertson sometimes stopped by the Hav-a-Java Cafe for a late lunch that was more like breakfast—a bagel and coffee. He was one of those people who don't think much about food—he was too busy to keep up with such details. Although he was always well dressed—nice suits, good ties—telltale mismatched socks or ink-spotted cuffs made it clear that he always had more important things on his mind.

Derek had been an engineer with Milletech Industries ever since completing his master's degree, and he was a fanatic about his work. If he was designing something, he lost track of everything around him. His car was often the last one in the parking garage at night and the first to arrive in the morning. People wondered if he went home at all. When totally focused on a project, he'd even forget to eat.

Lately, though, the rumors about the latest round of budget cuts at Milletech had made it difficult to concentrate. Derek's division, which produced the communication components for high-tech weapons systems, was likely to be downsized or even eliminated. The government wasn't buying the way it once had—there wasn't much need for research and development in his area anymore. His boss assured him that he would always have a job at Milletech, but he wanted more than just to have a job. He wanted to be excited by his job.

Even though Derek felt relatively secure in his job, as colleagues left for jobs in academia or moved to larger defense contractors, he was unsure about what to do. His work wasn't as engaging as it once had been—the thrill and challenge of design had faded over the years. More and more, his work was driven by the minute details of a microchip—most of what he produced these days was too small to be seen by the naked eye. The creative part of his job had disappeared

some time ago, though he was loathe to admit it.

A part of Derek hoped that his department would be eliminated. Then he'd have to make a change. He wanted to start looking, as he knew others were doing, but he just couldn't bring himself to do it. Instead, he started spending more and more time on his afternoon coffee breaks.

It seemed to be a sign when he got a call from Jeff, his college roommate whom he hadn't talked to in about a year. Jeff was heading up the marketing department at Signet Software. He'd gotten in on the ground floor at Signet and was one of the *wunderkinds* who had started their design division. Jeff told Derek about his job, how he was developing relationships with people in various fields and working out of a home office and keeping his own hours. He said that a lot of the people in Signet's marketing division were engineers and designers who also worked on projects on the side. Marketing sounded perfect—just the change Derek was looking for. Maybe there were jobs like that at Milletech. He could always count on his buddy for ideas.

The morning after his conversation with Jeff, Derek had gone into the office of his boss, Bob Justy, and told him he intended to bid for a marketing coordinator position in Milletech's new business communications group. Mr. Justy was taken aback, but gave Derek the approval he needed. Derek could hardly contain his excitement as he awaited his interview. He was positive that he would be making a great change. ✯

> *Derek could hardly contain his excitement as he awaited his interview.*

Ed at the Hav-a-Java Cafe would have been disappointed to hear how things worked out for his customers. Only Amanda was offered the job she interviewed for. Why were the others turned down? Were they not qualified? Or could they have done more to "sell" themselves to their interviewers?

START SPREADING THE NEWS: IDENTIFYING YOUR QUALIFICATIONS

2

Prove Your Worth by Giving Examples

Give STAR Examples That Match Your Skills to the Job You Want

Read a Sample Interview

Build Your STAR Repertoire

Practice Using STAR Examples

START SPREADING THE NEWS: IDENTIFYING YOUR QUALIFICATIONS

"It's not what you know; it's what you can prove," Dan said with a self-satisfied air. He had read it somewhere but thought it sounded original. And he was sure that it applied to Sara's situation, though he wasn't sure how.

Sara interrupted her assault on the banana split they were sharing long enough to sip a diet cola and nod with resignation. She knew she would have been perfect for this job—it was ***the*** job. And she had gone into the interview wearing her most professional-looking suit, carrying her attaché, and feeling confident in her ability to be a fabulous—what was it?—junior assistant account representative for the restaurant/hospitality division. But she had not managed to convince the company's president of that.

Sara could not understand why they hadn't offered her the job. Zwerner International Public Relations was the ideal place to work! She had sent in her best writing samples and aced all the tests they'd given her. But somehow she had blown the interview with Ms. Zwerner. Dan was great for buying banana splits and spouting maxims, but he wasn't helping her understand what went wrong.

Later Sara thought about the interview and about what Dan had said, "It's not what you know; it's what you can prove." Her samples and her tests had shown what she knew, but in her interview she hadn't proved herself up to the job. She remembered the interview as a series of long silences punctuated by her faltering responses to Ms. Zwerner's questions.

So she wasn't going to work at ZIPR. She was still up for positions at two other firms, Velovsky-Cromer and Billings, Umphrey, Taylor, O'Leary & Nelson. Her interview at Vel-Cro was coming up in three days. She began to replay the ZIPR interview in her mind and think about what she would do differently. Sara mimicked, "'Tell me about yourself.' What the hell kind of question is that? No wonder I couldn't come up with anything intelligent to say!" ✯

Prove Your Worth by Giving Examples

Dan's maxim did apply to Sara's situation. Sara had the knowledge and skills necessary to do a good job in public relations. Her experience on her college newspaper sharpened her writing skills, and her internship at an advertising agency gave her insight into creating a corporate image. Because her clients would have been major restaurant chains, even her experience as a waitress might have been useful. Sara mentioned these jobs in her interview, but she did not set out to prove that she had acquired the knowledge and could demonstrate the skills necessary to do well as a junior assistant account representative.

As you read the following excerpt from Sara's interview, look for opportunities Sara might have had to prove she could do the job. Mark these opportunities with a star.

Ms. Zwerner: So, Sara, why don't you tell me a little bit about yourself.

Sara: Well, I just graduated from the state university. I got my degree in comparative literature. I moved back here to live with my family while I find a job. I'm looking for something that will involve writing.

Ms. Zwerner: Well, this job certainly does require a lot of writing. Tell me, Sara, have you ever written professionally before?

Sara: Uh, no . . . I did write for my school paper, though.

Ms. Zwerner: Do you have experience in public relations?

Sara: No, I've never worked in PR. Last summer I had an internship at an ad agency that did some public relations work, but I wasn't really in that group.

Ms. Zwerner: Any other work experience?

Sara: Well, I was a waitress while I was in school, but that's really all.

Ms. Zwerner: Why did you decide to look for a job in public relations?

Sara: It was recommended to me by some of my professors—they thought my writing was good and this was a field that would make good use of that.

Ms. Zwerner: Why do you think you'd be a good match for this position?

Sara: Well, your company seems to be a great place to work. Everyone I've talked to seems very happy here, and they all seem to be doing a lot of creative work—just the kinds of things I'd like to be doing.

☆ ☆ ☆ ☆ ☆ ☆

Where did you place your stars? In fact, every question was an opportunity for Sara to prove herself. Sara missed most of these opportunities by answering questions in a tentative way, without offering proof of her abilities. What did Ms. Zwerner learn about Sara? Not much.

Sara mentioned her writing ability and creativity several times, but she talked about her skills in a general way. Sara assumed that her interviewer had read and remembered the writing samples she had attached to her resume. Her second assumption was that the samples reflected writing that was similar to the writing she would do in the position. These assumptions might or might not have been valid. Sara's answers focused on her general abilities and talent for writing, not on whether she would be a good match for the job.

When Ms. Zwerner asked, "Why do you think you'd be a good match for this position?" she hit on a concept that DDI uses in training managers and human resource professionals to select the best candidates to fill jobs within their organizations. The DDI method involves defining job requirements and then obtaining evidence of knowledge/skills, past behavior, or motivations that shows a match or a mismatch.

Making a good match means looking at mutual interests. The interviewer wants to find the best employee for the organization. The job seeker is looking for the best opportunity to build skills, grow a career, and engage in satisfying, enjoyable work.

Sara's answer to the question of why she would be a good match was on track, but she needed to say more. She spoke about why she'd like to work for ZIPR, but she didn't talk enough about what she had to offer and why she would be worth their investment in hiring and training her.

"What do you think that meant?" Sara asked Dan. "A good match?" They started talking about the old TV show, "The Match Game." The host would read part of a sentence, and each contestant had to finish it, recording the answer on a card. A panel of celebrities did the same thing. The contestants got points for matching what the celebrities had written. Sara remembered that the goal was not only to think of a good ending for the sentence, but to think of how the celebrities would answer.

Talking about the game show seemed like an unrelated conversation—something to take Sara's mind off her misery—but the comparison started to mean something to her. Sara realized that she had to think about presenting her skills in a way that would show not only that the job would be a great opportunity for her (and that she wanted it badly), but also that she could meet ZIPR's needs. "Maybe this is a little too much thinking," she decided, letting out a deep breath. ✯

Give STAR Examples That Match Your Skills to the Job You Want

Rather than get lost in Sara's "Match Game" analogy, let's consider how to answer interview questions effectively. The best way to demonstrate to an interviewer that you are highly capable of meeting the needs of the position is by giving examples of times when you've effectively used your skills to meet other similar needs. It's like writing a proof in geometry or building a legal case.

Even if you have limited work experience or if you've worked in a field different from the one you're applying for, you probably have many examples of times (at work, in school, as a volunteer) that you've come up with an idea, managed a project, exceeded someone's expectations, learned something new, or helped someone else meet a challenge. These are skills that would be valuable to almost any employer.

By discussing your skills and how you've used them effectively in the past, you lead your interview away from clichés such as, "I'm a hard worker," "I'm a people person," or, as in Sara's case, "I write well." Instead of generalizations that cannot be proven, you are giving your interviewer behavioral evidence.

DDI consultants train interviewers to ask questions that draw out specific examples of past behavior that are relevant to the positions they are looking to fill. The theory behind our method is a simple one: Past performance is the best predictor of future behavior. So, when a candidate gives an example of a time when she did something well, she is letting her interviewer know that she will be able to use that skill again.

Although Sara's interviewer didn't ask for specific examples, Sara had several opportunities to share behavioral data. When she began to think in terms of making a match between herself and the ZIPR job, she also began to see how she might have proven herself in the interview.

When Ms. Zwerner interviewed Sara, she looked for indications that Sara would do an effective job as a junior assistant account representative for the restaurant/hospitality division and that she could eventually be promoted to assistant account representative or even account representative. Ms. Zwerner was listening for indications that Sara had not only the ability to write (because the JAAR spends a lot of time working on detailed reports for clients), but also the ability to manage her time and juggle multiple assignments (things she would definitely have to do as an AAR) and a talent for satisfying customers (many of ZIPR's clients had a reputation for being demanding). An understanding of the restaurant/hospitality business would be a nice plus, but was not essential.

How could Sara have known what Ms. Zwerner was looking for? Several of the companies that Sara interviewed with had given her a job description to review. Job descriptions or postings usually list the day-to-day tasks associated with the position as well as other information, such as educational or experience requirements. Had Sara received a job description from ZIPR, she might have better understood the type of writing she'd be doing as a JAAR and who her clients would be. The job description might also have included information on promotion opportunities available to a JAAR.

Although she had no job description from ZIPR, Sara could have gathered this information by asking questions of people in the organization, such as the human resource associate who sent her a proofreading test or the restaurant/hospitality division manager who spoke with her briefly when she dropped off her writing samples. Even without this information, Sara had a general idea of what an entry-level PR job involved (writing, writing, writing), which she could have used to engage Ms. Zwerner in developing an accurate job profile.

Doing this kind of homework before an interview is very important. Most career counselors and job placement specialists spend a lot of time with their clients discussing background information on the company they'll be interviewing with and the specific position they'll be interviewing for. A nervous candidate often will cram facts about a company. A woman Sara met in the lobby at ZIPR had memorized the firm's entire client list. Facts are nice, but they won't produce a winning interview. The most important prep work you can do is to determine the requirements of the job and then plan how you can prove you meet those requirements by giving examples of your accomplishments.

Read a Sample Interview

Here's a look at how the interview might have gone. Let's imagine that Sara had taken some time to review her own resume, with an eye toward the information she had collected about the job, and thought about relevant experiences that demonstrated her talents. This time as you read the interview, mark with a star each piece of behavioral data that Sara gives.

Ms. Zwerner: So, Sara, why don't you tell me a little bit about yourself.

Sara: Well, I just graduated from the state university. I got my degree in comparative literature. As a comp lit student, I did a lot of reading and writing, mostly papers analyzing what I'd read. I found I have a real talent for making sense of things by writing about even the most complicated literature in a clear and simple way.

In one of my first comp lit courses, I had to write a term paper on allegorical figures in literature from India. I tried to think of a way to make the subject matter more engaging, so I used current popular figures, such as Madonna and Michael Jordan, to personify some of the figures I was writing about. My professor ended up using the same idea to introduce that material to his students the next semester—and I got an A+! I was proud that I was able to make an obscure topic both entertaining and understandable. I'm looking for a job that would allow me to use that talent.

Ms. Zwerner: Well, this job certainly does require a lot of writing. Tell me, Sara, have you ever written professionally before?

Sara: I was a reporter for my school newspaper, and two of my stories were picked up by other papers. I learned to work under the pressure of a deadline and to make use of the resources I had available to me. I often had to interview university officials who were reluctant to speak to a student journalist—particularly when I was writing about the effect that budget cuts were having on students who counted on university funds for research and scholarships.

I had to be both creative and persistent in order to get the information I needed to write my articles. For example, I did anything I could think of to talk with the university president. Several times I sat outside her door for hours. Once I even paid a person from a restaurant to let me deliver what she'd ordered for dinner. That convinced her to give me an interview. It was a great experience!

Ms. Zwerner: It sounds like it was a real challenge. Do you have experience in public relations?

Sara: Last summer I was an intern at an ad agency that did public relations work, and although I worked with the print media advertising group, I learned how advertising and public relations work together to serve clients.

For one account I helped prepare for the initial presentation. The buyer liked one of my ideas—the product was decaf coffee, and I suggested a humorous campaign using the tag line, "Like life isn't stimulating enough," and showing a person running to catch a train or finding out he had to make a presentation to an auditorium full of people. Anyway, the account executive allowed me to sit in on the presentation and help with the entire project, and I got to see my idea through from a rough concept to a whole campaign. The client was pleased that the agency had such a young approach—it helped them appeal to a new kind of consumer.

Ms. Zwerner: Sounds like you really learned a lot on that internship. Any other work experience?

Sara: Well, to make some extra money, I worked part-time as a waitress while I was in school. At first I didn't think of it as a "real" job—I didn't think I could learn anything by serving burritos—but just having a job while I

was a full-time student was a learning experience and a crash course in time management. Also, I developed a concern for customer service because I could see its benefits so clearly in the amount of tips I took home each night. Doing little things, such as sending someone to the corner store to pick up a paper so a customer could check movie times, paid off—not just in tips, but in building repeat business.

Ms. Zwerner: You've had a lot of different experiences. Why did you decide to look for a job in public relations?

Sara: I asked some of my professors for suggestions about jobs that would give me the opportunity to write and be creative. Several people mentioned public relations, and when I started doing research on jobs, I thought it was a good match too. Working on groups of accounts means managing multiple projects, and I enjoy having several things going on at once. My grades were the best when I was working and taking a full schedule of classes. Public relations is about helping the client get a message out to a specific audience. A successful message links what a company offers to what a customer needs. Making that link clear can be difficult, but it's similar to what I did in that paper on Indian literature that I mentioned earlier—I took a topic and made it something people could understand and relate to.

Ms. Zwerner: Why do you think you'd be a good match for this position?

Sara: Well, I think your company would be a great place to work. People seem happy and are doing creative work—just the kinds of things I'd like to be doing. I understand that this position involves making sure demanding clients stay informed of how we're managing their accounts. I'm confident that I could handle all the activities for an account and write clear, easy-to-understand reports for the client. What else should I know about this position?

☆ ☆ ☆ ☆ ☆ ☆

In this version of the interview, Sara gave Ms. Zwerner specific examples of behaviors she had demonstrated in the past and linked these experiences to how she would perform as a JAAR. Her responses showed that she had thought about what her responsibilities would be and who her customers would be.

Which of Sara's examples were most effective? Her examples about her paper on Indian literature and her interview with the university president gave the most information and were therefore the most persuasive. Examples such as these are the best kind of "proof" a job seeker can offer.

We asked you to mark your examples with stars because the information provided in our effective responses falls into a STAR format: Situation/Task (ST) explains the circumstances, Action (A) describes what the person did, and Result (R) describes the outcome of the action.

Situation/Task: Sara had to write a term paper on a complex subject—allegorical figures in literature from India.

Action: To make her paper more interesting, she used modern celebrities as a basis for comparison.

Result: Her paper was entertaining and readable. The professor adopted her idea for use in future classes and graded her paper A+.

Situation/Task: As a reporter for the university newspaper, Sara tried to get an interview with the university president, who was reluctant to discuss recent budget cuts that had angered students.

Action: Sara posed as a delivery person to gain access to the president's office.

Result: Impressed by Sara's ingenuity, the president granted the interview.

Giving examples in the form of STARs is the best way to prove yourself during an interview. Ideally, an interviewer will guide the discussion by requesting specific examples that deal with distinct job requirements. However, Ms. Zwerner asked Sara general, open-ended questions. In the actual interview Sara responded to these questions giving little behavioral data. In the second version of the interview, Sara responded to the same general questions with specific examples in the form of STARs. Later in this book, we'll discuss strategies for dealing with challenging interviewers, including those who ask vague questions.

A DDI-trained interviewer who wanted to check Sara's communication skills might have phrased a request like this: "Tell me about a time when you had to write or speak about something complicated or difficult to understand." Such a request would have made it easier for Sara to provide a STAR response. If she hadn't responded with behavioral data and had given a general response such as, "I had to write at least one paper on an obscure subject every semester," the interviewer would have probed further asking, "Can you think of a specific time when that happened?" or "Walk me through the steps you took in one situation." An interviewer who is seeking behavioral data will follow up in an area until several STARs are obtained or the interviewer is sure that the candidate doesn't have any more examples to share in that area.

No matter what kinds of questions you encounter in your interview, you can effectively

give examples of your skills by using the STAR format. In the exercise that follows, imagine that the interviewer is attempting to draw out behavioral data. The exercise includes both the interview questions and some hints on thinking through your answers.

Preparation Exercise

Build Your STAR Repertoire

The purpose of this exercise is to help you to begin thinking about the kinds of examples you would share with an interviewer. Read our example and then complete as many of the exercise items as you need to in order to get the feel of giving STAR responses. Our example contains a complete STAR as a candidate would relate it to an interviewer. We've captured exact wording in order to convey to you all the elements of a STAR. You, however, don't need to write in such detail to complete this exercise. You are the only one looking at your responses, so use key words, phrases, and abbreviations that mean something to you—just enough to jog your memory. Just be sure that when you're actually in the interview, you use clear and precise wording.

Example

"Tell me about a time when you went out of your way to satisfy a customer."

Situation/Task: I was working in the production department of a large publishing company. We received a letter from a nine-year-old girl who was unhappy because the gold design had worn off the cover of a book we had published. She wanted a refund. My boss gave the complaint to me to handle.

Action: I immediately requested a refund check from our accounting department. I also called our printer, who investigated and identified one run of books in which the covers had been improperly printed. I obtained a copy of the book with a properly printed cover, and sent the book, the refund check, and a personal letter to the girl, thanking her for pointing out the problem and apologizing for the inconvenience.

Result: The girl's mother called to thank me for the response. She told me that she was going to recommend our books to all her friends with children.

Build Your STAR Repertoire

Continuous Learning and Growth	Sales Ability
Continuous Learning and Growth: "Tell me about a time when you had to learn something totally new." Hint: Detail the steps you took to learn and tell how you applied what you learned.	Sales Ability: "Tell me about a time you tried to persuade a person or group to do something they didn't want to do." Hint: What was the situation? Why did people resist? What arguments were made?
Situation/Task:	**Situation/Task:**
Action:	**Action:**
Result:	**Result:**

Preparation Exercise

Build Your STAR Repertoire

Tenacity: "Give me an example of a time when you faced a lot of obstacles to achieving a goal." Hint: What were you trying to accomplish? What were some of the obstacles you faced? How did you address them? Were there some failures along the way? What were the steps you took to achieve your goal? How did things turn out?

Situation/Task:

Action:

Result:

Planning and Organizing: "Tell me about a situation (personal, academic, or professional) in which you were responsible for planning and organizing an event." Hint: How did you get the assignment? How did you approach the task? How did you keep track of things? What tools did you use (to-do list, organizer, etc.) to help you? What was the first thing you did? What steps followed? How did you feel when the event took place?

Situation/Task:

Action:

Result:

Build Your STAR Repertoire

Stress Tolerance	Leadership and Influence
Stress Tolerance: "Give me an example of a stressful situation you've experienced." Hint: What was happening? What made it stressful? Were you in the situation alone or with others? How did you interact with them? What did you do in this situation? Were you in control of events (for example, taking an exam), or did you require outside help (for example, being trapped in an elevator)? What did you do to manage your stress? How was the situation resolved? How did you feel afterward?	**Leadership and Influence:** "Tell me about a time when you guided individuals toward achieving a goal." Hint: Were you assigned as leader, or did you step up to the task? What did you do to make sure everyone worked together? What interpersonal challenges or conflicts did you face? How did you help people overcome them?
Situation/Task:	**Situation/Task:**
Action:	**Action:**
Result:	**Result:**

Preparation Exercise

Build Your STAR Repertoire

Initiative: "Tell me about a project or role that you've taken on that is outside your job description." Hint: Tell about a job or role that you changed substantially while you held it.	**Communication:** "I'd like to hear about a time when you had trouble seeing eye to eye with a colleague." Hint: Walk through the steps you took to resolve the problem.
Situation/Task:	**Situation/Task:**
Action:	**Action:**
Result:	**Result:**

Build Your STAR Repertoire

Teamwork/Building Partnerships/Collaboration: "Tell me about a time when you worked with a group or team of people to complete a project." Hint: Describe your role and what specific actions you took to ensure the project's success. What team problems arose, and how were they resolved? **Situation/Task:** **Action:** **Result:**	Decision Making: "Tell me about a time when you were faced with a difficult decision and describe how it turned out." Hint: What alternatives did you consider? **Situation/Task:** **Action:** **Result:**

Practice Using STAR Examples

How did you feel about this exercise? For some people, using the STAR format comes easily—it's like telling a story. For others, it's not a natural way to think about experiences. The best way to develop your skill at giving examples is to practice. The next time you're telling someone about what happened in a big game or on your favorite TV show, tell the story in the form of a STAR—describe the situation or task, tell what action was taken, and describe the result. It won't take long for you to get used to it!

The best way to develop your skill at giving examples is to practice.

You don't always have to relate your examples in the STAR sequence—first situation or task, followed by action, and then result. Sometimes it is clearer if you give the result first, followed by the situation or task and action. For other situations, your action is key and should come first, followed by the other elements. The order doesn't matter as long as you include all three pieces of information.

One note of caution: Because giving a STAR response in an interview is like telling a story, it can be tempting to stretch the truth or create an answer. Lying in an interview is never a good idea. Most likely, you will get caught! And even if you don't get caught, you might end up in a job for which you are ill suited or unprepared.

Remember that no one is perfect—it's unlikely that any one candidate will have terrific examples to share for every question. Instead of lying, draw on experiences both in and out of your professional life—the most recent examples are best, but a compelling story about how you handled your first job or a challenging school experience can illustrate a lot about your behavior too. Don't overlook volunteer work or activities within your place of worship. We'll discuss these types of examples in detail later.

NOTES

THEY SAY IT'S NOT WHAT YOU KNOW, BUT THEY'RE OFTEN WRONG: LOOKING AT YOUR KNOWLEDGE/SKILL DIMENSIONS

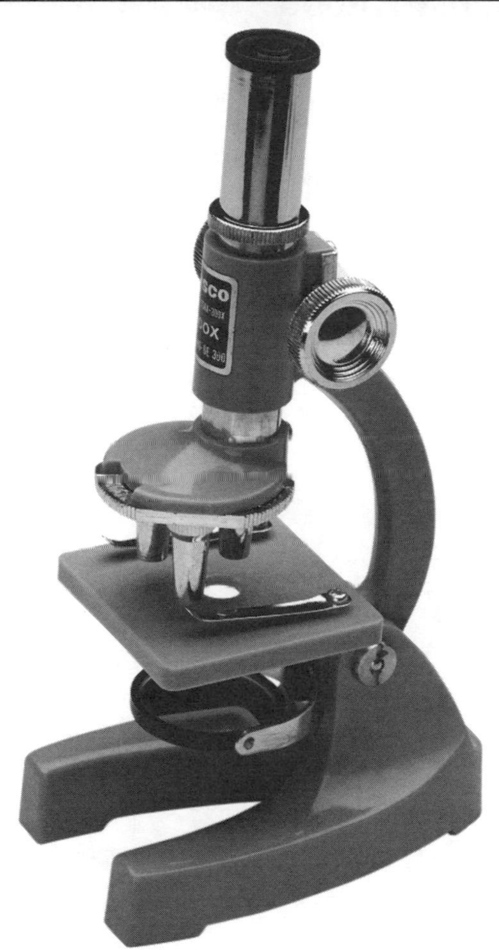

3

Identify What You Know or Can Do

Providing Evidence

Focus on the Practical

What About What You Don't Know or Can't Do?

You Can't Know Too Much

3 THEY SAY IT'S NOT WHAT YOU KNOW, BUT THEY'RE OFTEN WRONG: LOOKING AT YOUR KNOWLEDGE/SKILL DIMENSIONS

Tom saw himself as a confident guy, someone not easily intimidated. He spoke his mind, always had. In his 25-year career at GenEquip, he'd had gripes with top management—who doesn't?—but he never thought seriously about leaving. He didn't always sing the company song, but he liked his job and the people he worked with. He'd done well by GenEquip, and they'd done well by him. Besides, the alternatives were grim. A lot of guys he knew were taking pay cuts, and his next-door neighbor had just been laid off.

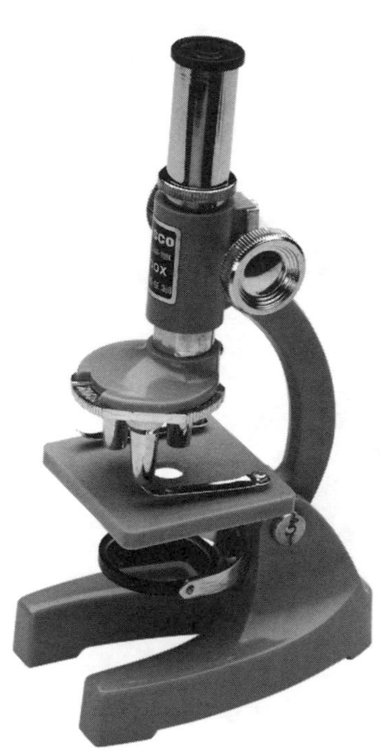

Tom's parents had always meant for him to go to college. He would have been the first one in his family. But his senior year had come and gone, and he'd never even applied. His little sister had gotten sick that year; money was tight, and it seemed as if a dark cloud were hanging over his house. How could he have thought about leaving for school?

He had never doubted that he'd done the right thing by graduating and going straight to work. Over the years he had looked into those schools—the ones that advertised on the radio—where a person could earn a degree by going to classes at night and on weekends. He told himself he'd get his degree eventually, once he found the time. But in the past 10 years, he'd managed to take only two classes.

But he knew something: Confident or not, he was scared as hell to go back to school. His grades had always been decent—better in math than in English. But that was years ago, and all that stuff had probably changed since then. And the thought of sitting in a classroom filled with 18-year-olds . . .

Tom flashed back to arriving at GenEquip's corporate headquarters for his interview and running into that guy in the lobby. Tom imagined him to be named "Harris" or "Parker"—no, it had to be "Charles." Like the prince. Charles, who had just come from an interview for the job Tom wanted. Charles, who would get that job because of his fancy degree. Not having a degree was Tom's Achilles' heel, and it was always coming back to trouble him. Before he had even set foot onto the eleventh floor of corporate headquarters, he was sure he wouldn't get the job.

And he was angry about it. He knew he was smart enough and had the right experience—few people understood the company and its procedures better than he did. He was certain he could do the job but knew he'd never get it—for lack of a damned piece of paper. It just didn't seem right.

When Tom met his interviewer, Edward Anderson, he thought the man looked as if he'd just stepped out of the pages of GenEquip's annual report. From the well-starched collar of his white shirt to the freshly polished wing tips, Mr. Anderson had looked every inch the corporate leader. Tanned and self-assured, he had presented the handshake of a man who was accustomed to impressing people. He was exactly what Tom was afraid of. ☆

Identify What You Know or Can Do

To Tom every question focused on his lack of a degree. He assumed that Mr. Anderson would be interested only in the extent of his "book learning" and wouldn't place much value on the skills he had learned on the job.

At one point Mr. Anderson had asked about Tom's project management skills:

Mr. Anderson: Obviously, this position is going to require project management skills. What methods have you studied?

Tom: I haven't had any course work in it—no formal education on management at all, really.

☆ ☆ ☆ ☆ ☆ ☆

Tom answered the question directly, but in doing so, he missed an opportunity. He might have answered by describing the project management he'd done at the plant and what he had learned from his experiences in different roles. What Mr. Anderson was looking for was some demonstration of Tom's knowledge and skill level in project management. We call this a knowledge/skill dimension.

By our definition a knowledge/skill dimension is what you need to know or be able to do to successfully perform a job. Strength in knowledge/skill dimensions is developed over the years by a combination of experiences, such as learning from mistakes, receiving instruction from a mentor or leader, or attending formal training or educational sessions.

Examples of knowledge/skill dimensions are driving a truck, performing open-heart surgery, or repairing an engine. Some knowledge/skill dimensions, such as driving a truck, are best demonstrated by a license or certificate. Others, such as performing open-heart surgery, must be demonstrated both on paper (medical school diploma) and in practice (internship in heart surgery).

Still other knowledge/skill dimensions can be demonstrated simply by doing. In other words, it doesn't matter if you learned to repair an engine in auto shop class or from your second cousin. If you can do it and do it well, that's enough. For such dimensions you might be expected to prove your knowledge/skill not only by giving STAR examples of a time when you used the skill, but also by performing the task or providing a detailed description of the process.

Even if you can support a knowledge/skill dimension by a certificate or degree, it is important that you are able to show that you can apply the dimension. For example, being a CPA is a good indication that you understand accounting. But a stronger indication would be the examples you can offer of difficult accounting assignments you have handled.

You don't have to have an MBA to understand cost accounting or economic projections. These and other skills can be learned through seminars, books, and internal (on-the-job) developmental opportunities. Often, you can learn or develop skills by being with people who are willing to teach you and allow you to practice under their tutelage. Many great chefs learn to cook at the side of other chefs rather than at formal culinary institutes. Many people easily use computer programs, although they haven't had formal training in them. Instead, they work through the programs until they develop enough skill to use the software at a productive pace.

For all types of knowledge/skill dimensions, from baking cookies to designing rockets, it is important to develop STAR examples of times when you've applied your knowledge/skill. They build your credibility and prove your case.

Preparation Exercise

Providing Evidence

The following pages give you the opportunity to record the knowledge and skills that you possess and want to present in an interview. We have provided hints about what to consider, but don't be limited by these suggestions and don't think that you have to fill in every section. Consider everything you have learned and every skill you have developed and then record those that are most important to future jobs.

Draw your STAR examples from specific applications of what you know. For instance, if you know how to use the program Microsoft® Excel, note how you used it to design an expense report, a monthly budget, or a profit-and-loss report, including specific information on the results of your actions. How accurate was the report? What value did it add to your department's budget planning?

Write no more than three STARs for each dimension you think is important. Often one strong STAR will be enough. For example, "I was a political cartoonist for five years for the *Hatfield Times* and won four awards from the Associated Press. One of my cartoons was reprinted in the *New York Times*."

Thinking about STARs helps you decide which of your skills are most important and prepares you to prove that you possess and have applied the knowledge or skills. List your own dimensions as needed.

Providing Evidence	
Technical Knowledge/Skills	★ **STAR 1**
(For example, using Word for Windows™ software, operating a Macintosh™ computer, or performing CPR)	

Preparation Exercise

Providing Evidence

★ STAR 2	★ STAR 3

Providing Evidence	
Professional Knowledge/Skills	★ **STAR 1**
(For example, having training in employee hiring, medicine, tax accounting, chemical engineering)	

Preparation Exercise

Providing Evidence

★ STAR 2	★ STAR 3

Providing Evidence	
Process Knowledge/Skills	★ **STAR 1**
(For example, using order fulfillment systems)	
Job-Specific Knowledge/Skills	★ **STAR 1**
(For example, installation of an intranet system in an advertising agency)	
Organization-Specific Knowledge/Skills	★ **STAR 1**
(For example, an organization's history, products, vision and values, etc.)	

Preparation Exercise

Providing Evidence

★ STAR 2	★ STAR 3
★ STAR 2	★ STAR 3
★ STAR 2	★ STAR 3

Focus on the Practical

When you talk about a topic you know well—especially something complicated—it's easy to slip into using "theoretical" language. If you hear yourself saying, "I think," "I believe," or "In general," stop speaking. Your goal is to provide specific information that will help the interviewer evaluate how you would perform in the job you want. Make your response practical rather than theoretical by giving a STAR example in which you describe how you successfully applied the knowledge or skill in question.

Even if your interviewer asks a general question (for example, "What do you know about quantum mechanics?"), you can provide a specific example in the form of a STAR. A response such as, "I've concentrated on several important quantum theories. When I was working on a new way of splitting the atom, I was able to . . . ," will answer the questions and help you "sell" yourself as a person who will make valuable contributions to the organization.

What About What You Don't Know or Can't Do?

As you prepare for your interview, you need not worry about which of your specific knowledge/skill dimensions to stress. Most interviewers ask very direct questions about the knowledge/skill dimensions required by a given job.

If you're asked a knowledge/skill dimension question to which your answer is a clear "no" (for example, if the interviewer asks if you can use a software program you've never even heard of), don't panic! Many organizations are less concerned with knowledge/skill than with your ability to learn. Technology changes so fast and organizations are becoming so specialized that it is rare for managers to encounter job seekers with complete sets of knowledge/skill dimensions. Thus, many organizations hire applicants who don't have the full range of required knowledge/skill, but have sufficient ability to learn and the initiative and motivation to act on that ability. We'll cover that topic more later.

The nature of knowledge and skills is changing so rapidly that future jobs will require knowledge and sets of skills that haven't even been identified today. In fact, you've probably picked up some new skills in the last few years that you don't even know you've learned. That's why it's worthwhile to actually write out your STARs in the preparation exercise. You probably have more job-related knowledge and skills than you realize.

You Can't Know Too Much

Many organizations have eliminated their management trainee rotation programs and the "assistant to the vice president" jobs that once served as a proving ground for college grads and applicants with little or no related experience. In today's "flatter" organizations, job seekers who want to break into a new field often begin in nonmanagement (or associate-level) jobs.

> *If you are concerned about being perceived as overqualified for the job you're seeking, be sure to explain why you're pursuing the position.*

If you are concerned about being perceived as overqualified for the job you're seeking, be sure to explain why you're pursuing the position. Your interviewer might not readily perceive your rationale and might be concerned that you are seeking the job out of desperation and will leave for another position as quickly as possible.

Whatever your reasons for seeking a position for which you seem overqualified, be prepared to discuss how you plan to use your higher level knowledge and skill later in your career or outside the job. Also, your interviewer might be concerned about how well you'll fit in with an existing team if your credentials are superior to those of your potential peers. Be sure to convey your desire to fit in and be a real part of the team.

There are cases in which interviewing for a job below your skill level makes sense. You might be seeking a job that uses little of your formal education, but is a stepping-stone to other positions within an organization. For example, a sales associate position in a growing retail chain could eventually lead to a job as a store manager. Or you might be trying to break into a new or challenging industry.

It's important to be honest with prospective employers about your qualifications: Most employers recognize that there's no such thing as "overqualified" anymore, and limiting the information you give an interviewer can often backfire. When you are being considered against other candidates, that information might well be a tiebreaker in your favor. Or you might win the lower level position you seek, but miss important developmental opportunities because your unique knowledge or skills didn't get into your personnel file. Candidates who are willing, for economic or other reasons, to accept positions for which they are overqualified soon might be considered for promotion by organizations that value "growing their own" associates.

NOTES

APPLY YOURSELF: BEHAVIORAL DIMENSIONS AND USING WHAT YOU KNOW

4

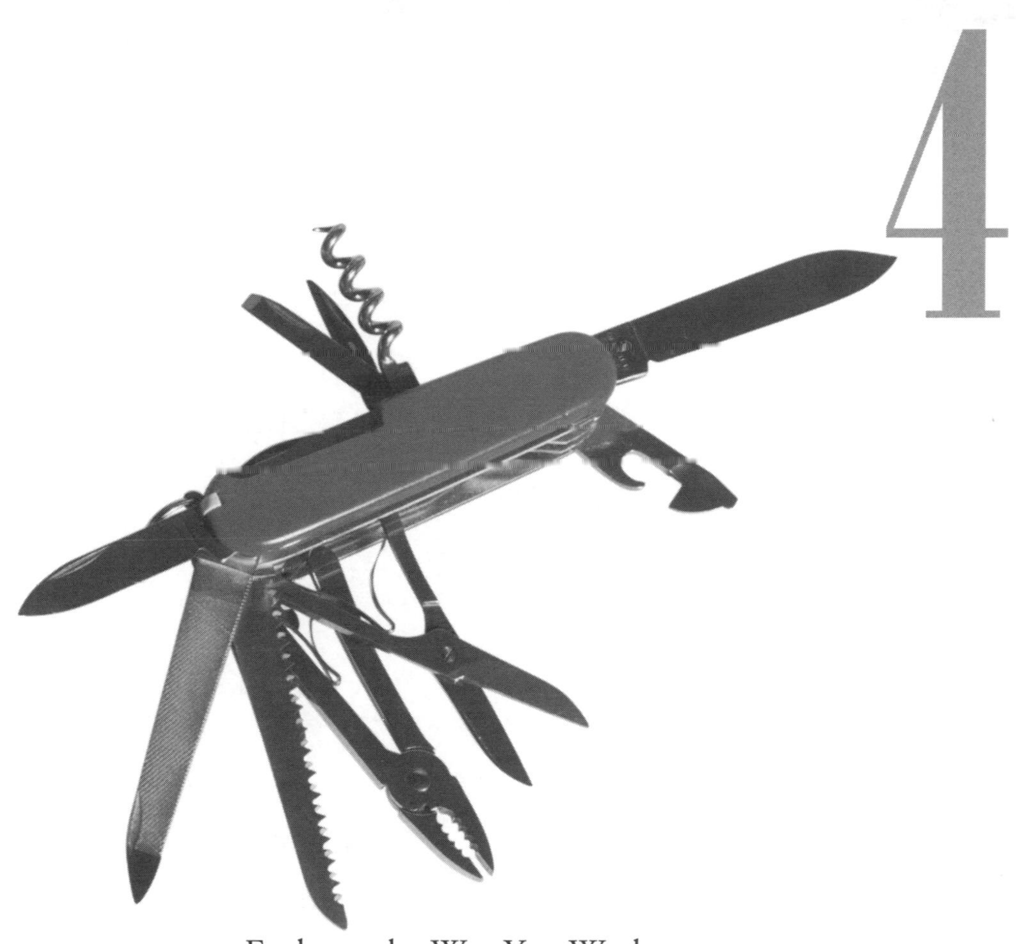

Evaluate the Way You Work

Identify Your Behavioral Dimensions

Develop Proof of Your Strengths

APPLY YOURSELF: BEHAVIORAL DIMENSIONS AND USING WHAT YOU KNOW

"I am having a really bad day," Tom announced to no one in particular. The woman sitting across the aisle from him flashed a pained smile and clutched her handbag. The man in the seat in front of him gave a grunting, humbug sound and turned to the next page of the sports section.

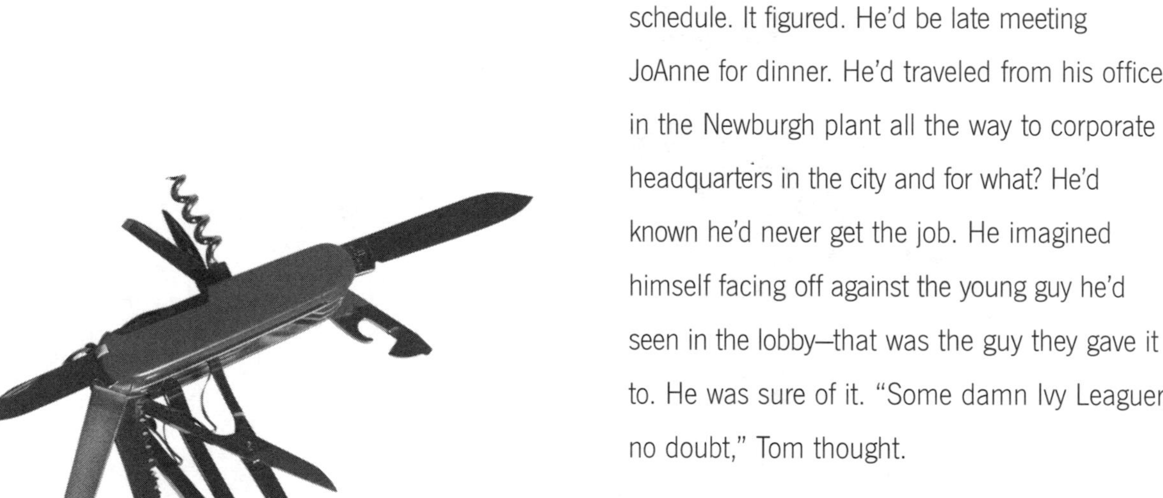

Tom's train was already 20 minutes behind schedule. It figured. He'd be late meeting JoAnne for dinner. He'd traveled from his office in the Newburgh plant all the way to corporate headquarters in the city and for what? He'd known he'd never get the job. He imagined himself facing off against the young guy he'd seen in the lobby—that was the guy they gave it to. He was sure of it. "Some damn Ivy Leaguer, no doubt," Tom thought.

Tom was angry at himself for even having tried for the position. He'd known it was a long shot. Joe would be disappointed in him. How would JoAnne feel? He shouldn't have gotten her hopes up. Twenty-two minutes late. Nothing to do but fall asleep and forget this whole, miserable day.

Tom opened a suspicious eye as someone's duffel bag knocked his elbow off the armrest. He rubbed his eyes. The train was nearly empty. He looked across the aisle to the window on his left. Summerville. He was only one stop from home. He must have been dead asleep.

He fumbled for his keys and thought about what he'd tell his wife. He'd handled the interview exactly as they had practiced, giving specific examples of past accomplishments in order to prove that he would do well as the project management team leader. He was sure that he had done his absolute best, and he was absolutely sure they hadn't picked him. He wasn't ever going to be one of those guys with an office in a high-rise building.

Shoulders stooped in disgust and resignation, Tom stepped off the train at Newburgh. ★

Evaluate the Way You Work

Before his interview Tom had thought through his in depth understanding of his company's products and processes. He planned to stress how important organizational and product knowledge would be for someone managing large projects.

The interviewer, however, was already familiar with what Tom knew. In fact, it was Tom's technical knowledge that had brought him this far in the interview process. Mr. Anderson was interested in finding out how Tom had applied what he knew. The application of skills—how you use what you know—is discussed in terms of behavioral dimensions.

The executives at GenEquip had been impressed with the results Tom had achieved during his tenure as a production manager at the Newburgh plant. Productivity was up, as was quality. Mr. Anderson was hoping to use this interview to learn about how Tom had achieved such impressive statistics. Specifically, he was hoping to find out about how Tom behaved as a leader, how he motivated others. Because success in the project management team leader position depended on collaboration and leadership without formal position power, Mr. Anderson wanted to gather information that would help him decide whether the way Tom managed people would work.

As you read Tom's interview, think carefully about his answers. Is he providing the information that Mr. Anderson is requesting?

Mr. Anderson: Tom, thanks for coming in today. I know you've got a tight schedule, so I've already reviewed your background. I'd like to learn about specific projects you've worked on at General Equipment and the skills you've developed over the years. First, I'd like you to tell me about a time when you were responsible for leading a group effort or project. Walk me through the steps you took to bring your team together and the specific things you did to keep them on track.

Tom: Just before I became a production manager, I was a supervisor in the main warehouse. I was assigned to lead the first process action team as part of our total quality effort. The production managers were concerned about the way that parts were piling up in the front of the warehouse before being stored. The storage areas are climate controlled, but up front the doors are often open, so some components were being exposed to the elements.

I decided to attack the problem by looking at the lifts that we use to transport the components to the storage areas. I wanted to see if the lift operators were being as efficient as they could be. When I started looking at all the numbers, I realized that one operator, Sandy, was consistently using less fuel and moving more components than the others.

At first I thought her machine must be more efficient than the other lifts, so I switched her to a different machine to see what happened. Using a different lift didn't affect Sandy's productivity. She still used less fuel and accomplished more work than the other operators. Watching Sandy work, I saw that for each load, she carefully planned her route through the warehouse, never needing to backtrack. She also did a maintenance check on her lift each morning, so she rarely had to stop during the day.

When the other lift operators started working this way, we were able to move the components more quickly and reduce their time in the open air. I think it really made a difference in quality—returns went way down that year.

Mr. Anderson: It sounds like you did great work. Tell me, Tom, what tasks did you assign to the rest of the team?

Tom: Well, the other supervisors in the warehouse were looking at other things in our processes, like our shift schedule, but sometimes they were able to help me with the adjustments I needed to make with the lift operators. Mostly, though, it was an opportunity for me to really understand the ins and outs of how we move and store our components.

Mr. Anderson: I see. Can you think of another time when you were responsible for leading a team?

Tom: After the success of our first process action team, we organized another one to see if we could decrease the time it takes to get completed components out to our distributors. Because other improvement efforts increased our production rate, we thought that reducing the time for this part of the process would be the next step in continuously refining production.

This time, I wasn't as familiar with some of the processes involved because I had just become a production manager. I had to read up on all of them and learn exactly what happens to a product after it leaves the assembly line and moves to the warehouse. After a couple of weeks, I understood it inside and out, and I was able to use the same technique I had used before—make refinements one step at a time to see what works. In the end we found we could reduce cycle time by only about an hour, but that hour has helped us out in a few cases. So I guess it was worthwhile.

Mr. Anderson: Sounds like another real improvement, Tom. Who else worked on that project?

Tom: Oh, there were a lot of people involved in production and distribution. I'd spend time with each person as I was working on learning and refining that piece of the process.

Mr. Anderson: OK, thanks. Tom, those were good examples. Now, could you tell me about a time when you were faced with a difficult or challenging problem at work and how you went about addressing it?

Tom: A few months ago our return rate started going up. It had fallen steadily since we'd begun our continuous improvement initiative, so I was surprised and concerned to see a jump.

At first, we couldn't figure out what was wrong with these components—whole batches were being returned. I started thinking about the new lubricant we were using on the switch-plates, and I wondered if that might have something to do with it. I knew that the lubricant can had warnings about not exposing it to high humidity. I decided to experiment. I took home two switchplates. One I put in the living room; the other I put in our bathroom. Sure enough, the one in the bathroom stopped working. It was the moisture. I switched back to our old lubricant on the assembly line, and we've had no problems since.

Was Tom providing the information the interviewer was looking for? Each time the interviewer asked about his experience with leading a team, Tom discussed his own efforts and what he had learned. Even when prompted to talk about others, Tom minimized their roles and discussed his own expertise.

Tom failed to listen closely to the interviewer's questions, which were clues about what was important for the position. Senior management was looking for a person who could lead a team—or several teams—in tackling an initiative that was too big for one person to manage.

Your behavioral dimensions—the way you use what you know in order to get things done—are central to your dimension profile.

Tom's knowledge of GenEquip as an organization was certainly a part of what made him a valuable employee, but even more important to his future success was his skill in assembling teams of other knowledgeable people and motivating them to solve problems. This ability—team leadership—is perhaps Tom's strongest behavioral dimension, yet he did not mention it in any of his answers to Mr. Anderson's questions.

Your behavioral dimensions—the way you use what you know in order to get things done—are central to your dimension profile. Information is constantly changing. The computer program you learned how to use last week might be obsolete within a year, but the way you learned it (your ability to learn new skills) makes you a valuable employee. A prospective employer probably won't be looking for you to generate reports that are exactly like the ones you had to complete in your most recent job, but your interviewer might be very interested in your talent for analyzing complicated data. Therefore, it's important that you be able to discuss your behavioral dimensions in an interview.

Preparation Exercise

Identify Your Behavioral Dimensions

The following pages show common behavioral dimensions and their definitions. Considering your experience in past and present jobs, which dimensions do you think best identify your strengths? Your areas of strength probably fall into three categories:

1. The behaviors you use every day. These are probably the dimensions that have been most critical to your job success, such as decision making or sales ability.
2. The behaviors that have produced long-term job success. These often relate to team leadership or interpersonal skills.
3. The behaviors you use occasionally (to complete monthly reports or organize a quarterly meeting) that have proven important to your success. You should have no more than three of these dimensions.

Considering the three categories just described, mark the dimensions you have chosen as your strengths with a corresponding 1, 2, or 3. Then write STARs for each. Remember, it's not necessary to write out the entire STAR example as you'd convey it in the interview. Just list key words or phrases.

Try to come up with three STARs for the dimensions you marked "1." For 2 and 3, think of as many as you can, but don't worry if you don't have three STARs for each. Even though these are important strengths for you, you might have fewer opportunities to demonstrate your abilities in these areas. Be honest with your interviewer and say that you'd like more opportunities to develop an area. Never invent an example and risk being labeled as dishonest or insincere.

You will undoubtedly have strengths in dimensions besides those listed in this exercise. You will have an opportunity to write STARs for these later. The purpose of this exercise is to help you understand behavioral dimensions and to start you thinking about your strengths.

Identify Your Behavioral Dimensions

Personal Dimensions

☐ Adaptability—Maintaining effectiveness when priorities change, when new tasks are encountered, and when dealing with individuals who have different views and approaches; effectively performing in different environments, cultures, locations, and when working with different technologies and levels of individuals.

☐ Building Trust—Instilling confidence and credibility through actions and communications.

☐ Continuous Learning and Growth—Assimilating and applying in a timely manner new job-related information that may vary in complexity; possessing intellectual agility needed to learn new concepts and tasks; showing eagerness and enthusiasm for learning news tasks and taking on additional responsibilities; taking the initiative in development activities; seeking and accepting feedback and coaching.

☐ Creativity/Innovation—Generating creative solutions that were implemented and made an organizational difference; questioning traditional approaches to work; accepting and encouraging the innovation of others.

☐ Energy—Consistently maintaining a high activity or productivity level; sustaining long work hours.

Preparation Exercise

Identify Your Behavioral Dimensions

★ STAR 1	★ STAR 2	★ STAR 3

Identify Your Behavioral Dimensions

Personal Dimensions

☐ Initiative—Asserting one's influence over events to achieve goals; self-starting rather than accepting passively; taking action to achieve goals beyond what is required; being proactive.

☐ Integrity—Maintaining and promoting social, ethical, and organizational norms; complying with company standards and ethical principles.

☐ Stress Tolerance—Maintaining stable performance under pressure or opposition (such as time pressure or job ambiguity); relieving stress in a manner that is acceptable to the person, others, and the organization.

☐ Tenacity—Staying with a position or plan of action until the desired objective is obtained or no longer reasonably attainable.

Interpersonal Dimensions

☐ Coaching—Facilitating the development of others' knowledge and skills; providing timely feedback to help them reach goals.

Preparation Exercise

Identify Your Behavioral Dimensions

★ STAR 1	★ STAR 2	★ STAR 3
★ STAR 1	★ STAR 2	★ STAR 3

Identify Your Behavioral Dimensions

Interpersonal Dimensions

- [ ] Communication—Expressing thoughts, feelings, and ideas effectively in individual and group situations (including nonverbal communication); presenting ideas effectively when given time for preparation (including use of visual aids); clearly expressing ideas in memoranda, letters, or reports that have appropriate organization and structure and correct grammar, language, and terminology; adjusting language to the characteristics and needs of the audience.
- [ ] Teamwork/Building Partnerships/Collaboration—Working collaboratively and cooperatively with others; building relationships; working effectively with team or work group or those outside the formal line of authority (e.g., associates, senior managers) to accomplish organizational goals; taking actions that respect the needs and contributions of others; contributing to and accepting the consensus; subordinating own objectives to the objectives of the organization or team.
- [ ] Valuing Diversity—Appreciating and leveraging the capabilities, insights, ideas, and efforts of all individuals; working effectively with individuals of diverse style, ability, motivation, or viewpoint.

Leadership Dimensions

- [ ] Leadership and Influence—Using appropriate interpersonal styles and methods to inspire and guide individuals (direct reports, peers, team members, and senior managers) toward goal achievement; modifying behavior to accommodate tasks, situations, and individuals involved.
- [ ] Meeting Participation/Leadership—Using appropriate meeting participation and facilitation styles and methods to guide participants toward a meeting's objectives; modifying behavior according to tasks and individuals present.
- [ ] Sharing Responsibility—Allocating decision-making authority and task responsibilities to appropriate subordinates; utilizing subordinates' time, skills, and potential effectively; creating a sense of ownership of job or projects by providing clear expectations, control of resources, responsibility, and coaching; offering help without removing responsibility.

Preparation Exercise

Identify Your Behavioral Dimensions

★ STAR 1	★ STAR 2	★ STAR 3

★ STAR 1	★ STAR 2	★ STAR 3

Identify Your Behavioral Dimensions

Decision-Making Dimensions

- [ ] Decision Making—Identifying and understanding issues and problems; utilizing effective approaches for choosing a course of action or developing appropriate solutions; taking action that is consistent with available facts, constraints, and probable consequences.
- [ ] Decisiveness—Making timely decisions, rendering judgments, taking action when appropriate, and committing to a side or position.
- [ ] Planning and Organizing—Establishing a course of action for self and others to accomplish a specific goal; planning proper assignments of personnel and appropriate allocation of resources.

Business/Sales Dimensions

- [ ] Customer Orientation—Effectively meeting customer needs; building productive customer relationships; taking responsibility for customer satisfaction.
- [ ] Global Perspective—Appreciating the opportunities and problems inherent in implementing organizational initiatives in countries/cultures around the world; taking into consideration marketing, manufacturing, distribution, and political situations in various countries when making decisions.
- [ ] Sales Ability—Using appropriate interpersonal styles and communication methods to gain acceptance of an idea, plan, activity, service, or product from prospects and customers.

Preparation Exercise

Identify Your Behavioral Dimensions

★ STAR 1	★ STAR 2	★ STAR 3

★ STAR 1	★ STAR 2	★ STAR 3

Develop Proof of Your Strengths

Writing these STARs helps you prepare what to say during an interview. Think of it as homework or prework for every interview you have. This kind of preparation and practice prevents you from drawing a blank, forgetting an experience, or failing to mention an event because you don't realize its significance.

This doesn't mean that you should prepare "canned" responses–you still need to answer the specific questions the interviewer asks. Preparation helps you explain and elaborate on your experiences and abilities and make clear connections between them and the requirements of the position you're seeking.

BEYOND METHOD ACTING: THE IMPORTANCE OF MOTIVATION

5

5 BEYOND METHOD ACTING: THE IMPORTANCE OF MOTIVATION

Amanda was sure she had the "look" right—it was very "New York," very "Audrey Hepburn." She was glad Jim was working the graveyard shift and hadn't seen her leave for work. She hadn't worn such a short skirt in years. She had bought the outfit—black wool suit with gold buttons, black hose, pumps, and handbag—especially for her first day of work. Though it was a gray day, she wore sunglasses; she liked the way they played off her red lipstick. It was the way she'd seen "fashion" people dress on television and the way the people she'd met on her interviews dressed. So what if this wasn't how she was used to dressing. A lot of things were about to change. Besides, she thought she looked terrific.

Amanda's brother-in-law often told her that looking right was half the battle—it's all about image, he would say. He was a lawyer, and when he talked to juries he knew that they had an idea about how lawyers were supposed to look and sound—the "Law & Order" thing. Sometimes he tried to create that image exactly (usually when the facts were on his side). Sometimes he played against it (when he was appealing to emotions) and came across as a "regular guy." Jim had grudgingly agreed with his brother's view of image, adding that most men didn't really know how to repair a car, but that every man knew how to open the hood and look around as if he knew what he was doing.

"If I act like I know what I'm doing," Amanda said to herself, "people will respect me and give me the help I need." She was visualizing what a competent fashion buyer would look like when the elevator doors opened on her floor. She took a measured step into the lobby of her new office. She didn't trip. So far, so good, she thought. She introduced herself to the receptionist, who directed her to an unoccupied desk.

An in-box, filled to overflowing, sat on the corner of the desk. At the desks around Amanda, people conducted animated phone conversations. The buzzing sound of a dozen people talking at once—a sound she had identified as excitement on her first tour of the office—seemed a lot more like chaos this morning. The desks were so close together—how could people hear themselves think?

On top of the in-box pile was a white booklet. It might have been a book report, with its austere, typed cover and single corner staple, but its title revealed it to be a description of the "Missy" department. Amanda began to read the report, which was filled with statistics about "Missy" customers. She read the same paragraph over and over, unable to concentrate above the noise around her or to forget the fact that no one had even said hello. ✯

Think About What You Like to Do and the Environment in Which You Like to Do It

Most people can relate to Amanda's anxiety as she faced her first day on the job. Entering a new environment, meeting new people, facing new expectations—beginning a job often means leaving behind your comfort zone, at least for a while. Nagging questions about your ability to perform or fit in can cause real self-doubt. It's probably not possible to assuage all those fears. Besides, facing and overcoming first-day jitters is an exhilarating part of starting something new. It is possible, though, to ensure that you like the job you interview for and are offered. Just as it's important to understand the knowledge and behaviors required in the job, it's equally important to be clear about motivational dimensions.

Just as it's important to understand the knowledge and behaviors required in the job, it's equally important to be clear about motivational dimensions.

Amanda thought she'd enjoy being a fashion buyer for Willowbee's because she enjoyed art and design and had an eye for clothes. During her first few weeks on the job, Amanda would indeed demonstrate her talent for buying. Unfortunately, she also would feel frustration about working in an informal, unstructured environment with little hands-on management.

During her interviews Amanda was tested for all the knowledge and skills she'd need as a fashion buyer and even for most of the behavioral dimensions she'd use. She wasn't asked, however, about her work style or about what motivated her, and she hadn't thought much about it either. In fact, although she was a match in behavior and knowledge, she was not a match in the motivational fit dimensions.

Think about what you liked best about your last job. Most people won't respond by mentioning a specific task ("I really liked putting together that monthly sales report"), but will point to the way something was done ("My team really worked well together; we got along, and we accomplished a lot"). These answers refer to your motivations, the way you like to get things done and the environment in which you like to work. If what you liked best

about your previous job was the way your team worked together, you ought to be looking for a job that embodies teamwork, not one in which you work alone in a remote field office.

Obviously, all jobs will have both positive and negative elements. The best job for you usually is one in which the positives outweigh the negatives. Sometimes, though, this might not be the case. For example, if you're trying to "break into" a particular industry, you might be willing to take a job with some unappealing aspects simply because the opportunity to gain experience is worth the sacrifice. You might make the same decision if you have an opportunity from a particular company or a job offer with a terrific salary. These choices aren't motivationally "wrong," but be clear that they are choices, and you have to live with them.

Opportunity for travel is an example of a motivational fit element that can require some deliberation. Few people with families are eager to spend more than half their work time traveling. Nights away from home can be an emotional burden for the traveler and can strain arrangements for those at home. For some people travel is nonnegotiable—no job is worth the burden of extensive travel. For others, it's something they're willing to accommodate. Many people find that with a few adjustments, their lives can run smoothly in spite of a hectic travel schedule.

We all make adjustments to our lives. For the super-organized, tardiness and disorder are hard to tolerate, but staying sane in a disorganized world often means living with a little messiness. When considering a job offer, think about what you can live with, what you're willing to try, and what is nonnegotiable. Your best job blends what you enjoy with what you are willing to live with. Always go into a job with your eyes open.

☆ ☆ ☆ ☆ ☆ ☆

As the alarm rang for the second time, Amanda's eyes fluttered open. Three weeks in this job, and she was dying for a vacation. Could she call in sick? It occurred to her that she didn't even know how. Who were you supposed to call? Was anyone keeping track? "It's a wonder anyone shows up," she muttered, as she sat up and stretched.

Her clothes were laid out on the rocking chair on the other side of the room; her coat, bag, and keys waited by the front door. She would do 30 stomach crunches, put on the coffee, and take a 10-minute shower. It was the same every day; exactly the way she liked it.

Drying her hair, Amanda flashed back to a conversation yesterday with Michael, the other new buyer who had started two months before she did. He seemed to be so happy with Willowbee's, and she'd wanted to know his secret. What was she missing?

"How do you know if you've done well?" she had asked Michael.

"You just know. And you'll get a sales report after the season is done. That will tell you."

"But don't you wish someone would tell you right when you've made a decision or right when you're about to, if it's a good one or not? Not somebody looking over your shoulder, but someone to give a little coaching."

"That would be someone looking over your shoulder," Michael had said. "And how would you develop your style if someone was constantly telling you 'yes' or 'no'? You just have to be a little more confident. I've seen the stuff you've chosen, and it looks great. Don't worry."

Don't worry, he had said. Hmm. How many new gray hairs had she counted in the last few weeks? She didn't understand how people could work with no structure, no guidance. She hurried back to the bedroom to finish dressing. She stopped herself, though, and thought: What would it matter if she was late? Who was counting? ★

Understand Motivational Fit

You might be wondering how Amanda's interview for the fashion buyer position went. The truth is that even when an interviewer asks the "right" questions (collecting behavioral data for the dimensions relevant to the job's day-to-day tasks) and the job seeker provides the "right" answers (STAR examples for those dimensions), a mismatch can occur. Many employers simply don't realize that motivational fit dimensions are important.

If motivational fit topics don't come up during your interview, it is in your interest to bring them up. Hiring a motivationally matched candidate is a win-win situation for both organization and candidate: The organization hires someone who will fit in, and the candidate feels satisfied working in the position. A motivationally matched employee is likely to be productive and committed. Letting a prospective employer know how likely you are to fit in has several benefits for you: You save yourself the misery of having a job you hate, and you are perceived as someone who is thinking about the "big picture" of the job and organization.

You can explore motivational fit when an interviewer gives you a chance to ask questions. You might ask about the environment—is it team oriented? Competitive? Fast paced? What kind of supervision or coaching will you receive? How will your performance be rewarded or evaluated?

If you can, have lunch with current employees as another opportunity to explore motivational fit. Amanda might have gotten a feel for the buyers' environment if she'd spoken with Michael beforehand and heard how the organization was meeting his preference of not having anyone "look over his shoulder." This might have prompted Amanda, who values structure and feedback, to ask one of her interviewers about the kind of coaching she could expect as a new employee.

There are actually three specific motivational fit dimensions: job fit, organizational fit, and location fit. Job fit relates to whether the specific position is a fit for you—does this job involve doing a lot of the things that you most like to do and few of the things that you least like to do? Most people think of job fit when they hear "motivational fit."

Equally important, though, are organizational and location fit. Organizational fit means that your working style and values mesh with those of the organization. The kind of environment you like to work in, the way you set your goals, the way you manage your time, the speed of decision making, the degree of empowerment, the need to take risks—these are all values that differ widely for people and organizations.

Any organization you interview with will have a culture—the sum of its values, the way things are done. In evaluating organizational fit, examine how well you'll be able to work within the existing culture of your potential employer.

When considering whether you'll fit well in a given organization, consider also where the organization fits into your career goals. Is it a stepping-stone to something better? Are people in this position often promoted or transferred? If so, how long does it take? Was the last person who held this position promoted? Are you in the industry you prefer to work in, but not in the ideal position? Would you like eventually to be doing this job for another company (perhaps a larger or more prestigious one)? These factors might help you decide whether potential negatives are worth enduring.

Finally, there is location fit. In some cases determining whether a position fits your location needs is as simple as answering one question: Can you relocate? No matter what your status—single, involved in a committed relationship, a parent—deciding whether to relocate can be agonizing. Is the job worth leaving your familiar surroundings? Can you handle a major life change along with a job change? There's no formula for making this decision, no right or wrong. Moving can be exhilarating or dreadful. And it's often both.

Location fit is an issue even for those who don't have to move. People who live in or commute to large cities must consider bus and train schedules, traffic patterns, and parking issues. Such factors might seem minor, but can produce major hassles.

In certain industries and job categories, location fit is becoming less important. As technology makes telecommuting (working from home and communicating with colleagues by phone, fax, and computer) a viable option, an increasing number of professionals are able to choose jobs without significant location fit worries.

Keep in mind these three aspects of motivational fit as you complete the following exercise.

Preparation Exercise

Analyze Your Own Motivations

Job Fit

Answer the following questions as they relate to your present or most recent job.

What kinds of things do you complete well in advance of deadlines?		What things in your job do you like to do least?	
What	Why	What	Why

What kinds of things do you tend to put off doing?		What things in your job do you like to do most?	
What	Why	What	Why

Analyze Your Own Motivations

Organizational Fit

Answer the following questions as they relate to your present or most recent job.

What behaviors does your organization value (who is rewarded, recognized, etc.)? Are the behaviors important to you?

Valued behavior	Importance to you (1-5)

What do you like most about your work environment?

Who are the most successful people in your organization? How do they think and work? Would you want to think and work the way they do?

Valued behavior	Importance to you (1-5)

What do you like least about it?

Preparation Exercise

Analyze Your Own Motivations

Location Fit

Answer the following questions.

Why or how did you choose to live where you do?

What personal responsibilities or desires make a location more attractive (for example, to live near children or parents)?

Personal factor	Importance to you (1-5)

What are your own or your family's health or educational considerations/needs that might be affected by location?

Health/Education factor	Importance to you (1-5)

What will change for you in the next few years that will affect where you want to live (for example, last child leaving home)?

Do you have to work around schedules (for example, for family meals or care of a child or aging relative)? If so, what are they?

What do you like to do that is affected by location (for example, water skiing)?

Like to do	Importance to you (1-5)

Motivational Dimensions Defined

Sometimes managers hire to redeem their last failures. If the person who most recently held a position tried to supervise colleagues without having the right or authority to do so, then an interviewer often will focus on finding a replacement who does not have a strong need for power. It's human nature to do this, and it explains some of the questions you'll encounter in your interviews. For example, a manager who has just fired someone for being constantly late might talk about punctuality during a significant portion of the interview for a replacement. Often in such a situation the manager might fail to look for other equally (or more) important factors that relate to job success.

You, the job seeker, can make the same mistake. You might want your next job to include characteristics, or facets, that aren't present in your current job, without really being sure about what you want or if what you're looking for will make you happy. For example, you may be searching for a job that involves leading other people because leadership was absent from your last position, without considering whether you are prepared to take responsibility for all the accountabilities that come with a leadership role. Or you might be swayed by "false positives." Does it really matter that your office is located next to a magnificent ski slope when you've avoided skiing for 30 years?

Because a job hunt can be fraught with emotion, it's important to do some in-depth thinking before your interviews and before you make decisions. The preparation exercises in this chapter have been designed to help you do just that. The answers you gave in the preparation exercise on pages 67-69 should start you thinking about the three areas of motivation. How might you characterize your responses? In the following exercise we have provided you with lists of the motivational facets we have found to be most related to job success and satisfaction. You should mark each facet in one of three categories (strongly like, neutral, strongly dislike) based on how important the facet is to you. Classifying the facets in this way will help you identify the ones most important to your job decision.

The preparation exercise beginning on page 71 will help you further by preparing you to communicate information about your motivations to your interviewer at the appropriate time. Feel free to add additional facets. The names you give the facets are not important—they should simply be meaningful to you. Sometimes a few words are enough. Sometimes you'll need to develop a short definition.

Preparation Exercise

Classify the Facets

Job Fit

The following list shows aspects of job fit that relate to a person's appropriateness for a position. Place a check mark in one of the columns on the right, based on your feelings about the item.

	Strong like	Neutral	Strong dislike
Opportunity for achievement	☐	☐	☐
Being the center of attention	☐	☐	☐
Chance to help/coach others	☐	☐	☐
Pay linked to output (commission)	☐	☐	☐
Complex tasks	☐	☐	☐
Opportunity for continuous learning	☐	☐	☐
Creativity required	☐	☐	☐
Handle details	☐	☐	☐
Follow exact directions	☐	☐	☐
Decisions based on diverse perspectives	☐	☐	☐
Fast work pace	☐	☐	☐
Formal recognition	☐	☐	☐
Participative decision making	☐	☐	☐
Technical orientation/rewards	☐	☐	☐
Independence	☐	☐	☐
Frequent interactions	☐	☐	☐
Interpersonal support	☐	☐	☐
Leading others	☐	☐	☐
Managing others	☐	☐	☐
Balance of work	☐	☐	☐
Holding position power	☐	☐	☐
Amount of pay	☐	☐	☐
Other ________________	☐	☐	☐

Classify the Facets

Organizational Fit

The following list shows aspects of organizational fit that relate to a person's appropriateness for a position. Place a check mark in one of the columns on the right, based on your feelings about the item.

	Strong like	Neutral	Strong dislike
Participative management (empowerment)	☐	☐	☐
Trust	☐	☐	☐
Customer service	☐	☐	☐
Openness to change	☐	☐	☐
Open communication	☐	☐	☐
"Ready, fire, aim"	☐	☐	☐
Innovativeness, change, creativity	☐	☐	☐
Security	☐	☐	☐
Equity	☐	☐	☐
Cooperation (among different parts of the organization)	☐	☐	☐
Product quality	☐	☐	☐
Caring for people	☐	☐	☐
Success orientation	☐	☐	☐
High risk/High gain	☐	☐	☐
Emphasis on planning	☐	☐	☐
"Lean and mean"	☐	☐	☐
Concern for short-term profit	☐	☐	☐
Decentralized organizational structure	☐	☐	☐
Risk taking	☐	☐	☐
Continuous improvement	☐	☐	☐
"Feast or famine"	☐	☐	☐

Preparation Exercise

Classify the Facets

Organizational Fit

	Strong like	Neutral	Strong dislike
High-technology orientation	☐	☐	☐
Growth at any cost	☐	☐	☐
Intellectual atmosphere	☐	☐	☐
Other ______________________	☐	☐	☐
Other ______________________	☐	☐	☐
Other ______________________	☐	☐	☐

Classify the Facets

Location Fit

Depending on the values and needs of the individual, the location of a job can be just as or more important than the responsibilities and tasks of the job. The following list shows location fit considerations. Place a check mark in one of the columns on the right, based on your feelings about the item.

	Strong like	Neutral	Strong dislike
Availability of special education programs	☐	☐	☐
Proximity to family members	☐	☐	☐
Commuting time	☐	☐	☐
Nearness of cultural organizations and activities	☐	☐	☐
Access to athletic/fitness facilities	☐	☐	☐
Public transportation availability	☐	☐	☐
Housing options and costs	☐	☐	☐
Desirability of climate	☐	☐	☐
Proximity to restaurants	☐	☐	☐
Proximity of athletic events	☐	☐	☐
Nearness to health care facilities and providers	☐	☐	☐
Shopping options	☐	☐	☐
Quality of public schools	☐	☐	☐
Religious institutions available	☐	☐	☐
Ability to take night classes nearby	☐	☐	☐
Cost of living	☐	☐	☐
Safety	☐	☐	☐
Ethnic/Cultural Mix	☐	☐	☐
Other ______________________	☐	☐	☐
Other ______________________	☐	☐	☐

Preparation Exercise

Prepare to Discuss Motivation

Consider job fit and organizational fit and identify up to five aspects you would want to be part of your job and five you would like to avoid. Think about the things that really motivate or demotivate you and list them at the appropriate places on pages 76-84. Don't worry about using our terms and definitions; use words that have meaning for you. Use the lists on the previous pages to spark your thinking. Check the preparation exercises on pages 67-69 to be sure that you have covered everything. You also might want to refer to the thoughts you wrote down in the introductory exercise on page xii.

After you've identified these motivators and demotivators, in the space provided write three STARs that demonstrate how you have experienced each and describe how each has had an impact on your job performance, career, or life choices. Think of specific incidents at work or elsewhere in which you've felt either highly motivated or strongly demotivated. What details about the situation would be relevant to your interviewer? We've provided some examples; write your lists and STARs below them.

<table>
<tr><th colspan="2">Prepare to Discuss Motivation</th></tr>
<tr><td>Job Fit</td><td>★ STAR 1</td></tr>
<tr><td>Motivators

Creativity</td><td>As a one-person graphics department, I worked on a variety of projects and had no one looking over my shoulder. I designed some innovative brochures, which won design awards.</td></tr>
</table>

Preparation Exercise

Prepare to Discuss Motivation

★ STAR 2	★ STAR 3
I volunteered to design the ads for a local theater group. I took a whole new direction with them, did some things that were very different, and attracted a lot of attention. Because of the publicity generated by the ads, all the performances sold out.	I developed a template for creating simple graphic elements. Others in the company were then able to do simple designs that had previously taken up a designer's time.

Prepare to Discuss Motivation	
Job Fit	★ **STAR 1**
Demotivators Fast work pace	A brochure I worked on had many last-minute changes. I was so rushed that I missed some of the changes, and the piece was printed with incorrect information.

Preparation Exercise

Prepare to Discuss Motivation

★ STAR 2	★ STAR 3
Every time I have to rush to meet a deadline, I go home with a headache.	I have trouble coming up with ideas if I'm put on the spot. My best ideas come when I have time to think. For example, when a vice president dropped by and asked for ideas on illustrations for a presentation, I couldn't come up with anything. Later in the day, though, I sketched out several ideas.

Prepare to Discuss Motivation	
Organizational Fit	★ **STAR 1**
Motivators *Openness to change*	*After years in a retail environment, I went back to school to train in graphic design. I've been much happier doing that kind of work.*

Preparation Exercise

Prepare to Discuss Motivation

★ STAR 2	★ STAR 3
I had 3 managers in 2 years—each asked me to make changes to the official presentation format. It was hard work, but the reasons for the changes made sense. As long as I understood the rationale, making the changes was interesting.	When I worked in retail, my manager encouraged me to make suggestions for improvements. She listened to everything and acted on many suggestions. I always felt like I was contributing something important.

Prepare to Discuss Motivation	
Organizational Fit	★ **STAR 1**
Demotivators *Concern for short-term profit*	*One of my managers refused to invest in a new computer system even though it would have improved the quality of our graphics.*

Preparation Exercise

Prepare to Discuss Motivation

★ STAR 2	★ STAR 3
The retail store refused to improve employee benefits and lost a lot of experienced workers—including me.	*An internal client wanted a complex brochure, but refused to budget for the printer with the expertise to do the job right. The result was a mediocre booklet.*

Prepare to Discuss Motivation

Location Fit

For location fit, list the five considerations that are most important to you and the five that might cause you to refuse a job offer. Again, examples have been provided.

Motivators

Suburban location with available parking

1.

2.

3.

4.

5.

Demotivators

Long commute

1.

2.

3.

4.

5.

Find a Comfortable Fit

What do you do if you find that things you listed as demotivators are part of the position you're considering? Job fit issues can change and improve over time. Many people destined for supervisory and managerial jobs start out in mundane positions. Incumbents feel that they can put in their time in these jobs in order to, down the road, obtain ones with a better job fit.

> *Organizational fit probably won't change over time because it is a product of deeply held corporate values.*

Organizational fit probably won't change over time because it is a product of deeply held corporate values. Any manager who has tried to change basic organizational values knows it's a huge challenge. A go-go, shoot-from-the-hip, ready-fire-aim organization is not likely to change to a deliberating, risk-avoiding organization any time soon. So, if an organization's values don't fit you, you are wise to avoid it in the first place.

Location fit might or might not be changeable. In many organizations, a new employee can expect to move from one location to another, with some locations being more attractive than others. In other cases, you might have to work in a particular town or not work for the company at all—it might have only one location or only one that's hiring. In thinking about location fit, you can get lost in wishful thinking. How nice that your office is located near a golf course, but if the job doesn't allow you the time to play golf, the location might be more of a negative than a positive.

Until now, we have focused on the extremes—things that, if present, would cause someone to be happy and things that, if absent, would make someone unhappy. The reality, of course, is that many aspects of the job are neutral.

An example of a neutral facet is the availability of free airline travel even though your family situation doesn't allow frequent travel outside the local area. In such a situation, the availability of this perk should make little difference to your job decision. Don't be overly influenced by the presence or absence of these nonrelevant motivational facets, regardless of how they are presented to you. It usually is enough to seek a good fit on the relevant facets without worrying about the ones that aren't very important. You are the expert on what motivates you.

NOTES

ARTIST'S IMPRESSION: PROFILING THE DIMENSIONS OF A JOB

6

Making a Match

Sketching a Job's Dimension Profile

Profiling the Job You Are Seeking

ARTIST'S IMPRESSION: PROFILING THE DIMENSIONS OF A JOB

Expressionless, Amanda sat on the train not feeling quite herself. In the mornings she used her commuting time to catch up on sleep. During the trip home she usually took the time to read. This evening she simply stared into space, paralyzed by her situation. Not having a job had been miserable, and now she was miserable in the job she'd taken. When she was at work, she wished she were at home. At home she could think of little besides work. Why did she feel like she was failing?

She couldn't imagine how things had gone so wrong. A job as a department store buyer had seemed perfect—who could resist being paid to shop? The people she'd met on her interviews had seemed very nice. But every morning she dreaded facing another day; every night thoughts of mistakes she was sure she'd made disturbed her sleep.

The train lurched forward in fits and starts; it was another 20-minute-delay kind of a day. "Let your mind go blank," Amanda said to herself. "Breathe deeply and relax."

But stray thoughts continued to fuel her imagination: herself 20 years in the future, still sitting at the same desk, older, hard of hearing, struggling to listen to someone on the telephone, but missing an important conversation; a riot in the Lady Willowbee department when she mistakenly orders only minidresses; a gaggle of older women spot her and give chase, wielding clutch purses and mismatched umbrellas; a warehouse full of double-breasted suits in chartreuse.

Since taking the job, Amanda had breathed, eaten, and slept Willowbee's Department Store. Mostly, she ate—Amanda was sure she'd gained 10 pounds. At night, plagued with dramatic images of her failure as a buyer, she curled up, sleepless, on the couch with sugar cookies and herb tea. She'd fall into bed in the early morning hours and be barely able to rouse herself when her alarm sounded at 6 a.m.

In spite of her exhaustion and the rocking motion of the train, Amanda could not make herself fall asleep. She tried thinking of nothing, then tried counting sheep. She hummed a lullaby and pictured herself on a tropical beach. Nothing worked. She was still there on the slow-moving train, heading home and thinking about what a disaster her day had been. It started when one of the distributors had changed his terms—suddenly the minimum order amount had jumped from 100 dresses to 500. How was she supposed to react to that? And then an order for fall was delayed. It wouldn't even ship until September 1. She sought advice from fellow buyers, who contradicted one another. She asked for coaching from her manager, who told her to "hang tough."

But Amanda couldn't hang tough—not much longer. The job felt impossible to master; each day brought a new crisis. And she had no one to help her. She couldn't complain to Jim; he wasn't thrilled with her going back to work in the first place, and she didn't want him to think she'd made the decision lightly. ✭

Making a Match

Amanda hadn't made her decision lightly, but neither had she gathered all the information she could have. After she'd finally made the decision to look for work outside her home, Amanda was so eager to get started that she was willing to take almost any position at all. Amanda really didn't know enough about the buyer's job to know whether it was a match or not. She had not sketched its dimension profile.

Amanda's problem is a poor dimension match. People are not qualified or unqualified in a general sense—it's the quality of their match with a specific job that counts. For example, a highly successful salesperson might do poorly as a sales manager because of a lack of leadership skills.

Mismatches can happen in any of the dimension areas. In Amanda's case the mismatch was between the motivational facets of the organization—the lack of nurturing, the fast pace—and Amanda's need for coaching and support. Motivational dimensions are the most commonly mismatched of the three types of dimensions.

To determine a match, your first task is to sketch a profile of the job you want by determining its dimensions in each of the three areas: knowledge/skill, behavior, and motivation.

Sketching a Job's Dimension Profile

What you need to know	Source of information
Job's knowledge/skill dimensions	Job title, job description, early interviews
Job's behavioral dimensions	Appendixes A and B, job description, early interviews, newspaper and magazine articles
Job's motivational dimensions:	
Job fit	Early interviews, observation of environment, job description, coaching from inside the organization
Organizational fit	Coaching from inside the organization, observation of environment, newspaper and magazine articles, organization's reports and brochures
Location fit	Early interviews

Most job descriptions explicitly state the knowledge/skill dimensions required for a job. For example, a description might include a list of equipment, tools, and computer hardware and software that must be used in performing the job. Minimal certification or education requirements also appear on the job description, such as "must have valid driver's license" or "BA required, MA preferred." Knowledge/Skill dimensions are frequently discussed during the interview process as well.

Some job titles, such as "systems engineer," have knowledge/skill dimensions that are easy to anticipate because they don't change much between organizations. However, job titles are becoming more generic, and employees have titles like "team member" or "project associate." In this kind of situation, you will have to do more research to define the knowledge/skill dimensions.

Because knowledge/skill dimensions are constantly changing and the skills that won you the job in the first place might soon be obsolete, it's likely that behavioral dimensions will be the main focus of your interview. Appendixes A and B list behavioral dimensions common to most of today's jobs.

A job description often won't explicitly list behavioral dimensions required for a job, but the description might be a useful tool in predicting them. A job description focuses on the output of a job or function—what the employee produces. How things are produced, how the employee generates the necessary results—these are the behavioral dimensions important to the job. Reading the appendixes in this book after looking at a job description should help you make an educated guess as to the most important behavioral dimensions for the job you are seeking.

To confirm your guesses, you can collect more data by using your interviews to ask specific questions regarding the dimensions you think are key to the job. It's more than acceptable to be direct with your questions: "I would think that communication skills would be very important to this job. Is that correct?"

You might even ask the interviewer for STARs. For example, if you are interested in how large projects are handled by the organization, you might ask for a specific example—how a project was identified or qualified, who was involved, what resources were used, what process was followed, etc.

The typical way that candidates gather information about organizations they'd like to join is simply by doing research. Scan the popular and industry presses for articles about the company. Are they announcing new priorities or initiatives? Are they downsizing and focusing on stock value? Are they involved in a merger that will require employees to form partnerships with their counterparts from another company? This information might give you some clues as to the behavioral dimensions interviewers will be looking for in a new employee. However, be sure the article deals with the unit of the organization you will be joining. In a large corporation the jobs and cultures of regional offices or divisions are often quite different from one another. Take care to research the part of the organization you'd like to join.

Of the three dimension areas, motivational dimensions are the most difficult to determine before your interview.

Of the three dimension areas, motivational dimensions are the most difficult to determine before your interview. During the interview, asking questions about motivational facets in which you perceive a mismatch is appropriate.

It's perfectly acceptable to ask to go to lunch with an individual from the department in which you'd like to work. An informal discussion with a potential peer can provide much information about how an organization really operates.

You can gather information indirectly by observing the work environment. At what pace are people working? What kinds of messages are displayed on bulletin boards? How do people treat you and one another?

Another effective way to gather information on the dimensions for a job is to find and talk with a person inside the organization who is willing to coach you. If the job you want is within your present organization, this should be fairly easy. Use your contacts in the department you would like to join. Ask about what it's like to work on that team, who is rewarded for what, etc.

This is a lot tougher to do if you're entering a company from the outside. Think about people you have met through another association, such as your place of worship, your community sports league, or a professional organization, who might be willing to coach you on at least some of the things that are important to know and do. But unless they work in the same department where your prospective job is located, internal coaches might have more information about organizational fit than about the specific facets of the job you want.

Preparation Exercise

Profiling the Job You Are Seeking

Use the forms on the following pages to list the dimensions that you feel are most important to success in the specific job you are seeking. List the dimensions in order, with the first one being the most important or most frequently used. Try to keep the list as short as possible—15 is optimum, but no more than 20. To help you with the behavioral dimensions, we have listed the most common behavioral dimensions (and their definitions) in Appendixes A and B. For now, fill in only the far left column under the heading "Dimension." In the next chapter we'll revisit this exercise as you match your dimensions to those required by the job you want.

You might be unsure of some of the dimension areas. For these, an educated guess is better than no guess at all. A profile is a starting point; during your job interviews you can add or delete dimensions as you improve your understanding of the job.

You should develop similar lists of dimensions for other jobs you are considering.

When you don't have time or you know nothing about the job for which you are interviewing, assume that the "Big Five" behavioral dimensions in Appendix C are important to the job and prepare STARs for them. DDI research indicates that they are the most commonly sought behavioral dimensions in today's jobs.

Profiling the Job You Are Seeking				
Dimension	**STARs: Recent, Job Related, Demonstrate Mastery/ Improvement**	**Rating 1 = Low; 5 = High**	**Shining?**	**Best Match?**
Knowledge/Skill Dimensions				
	★ **STAR 1**			
	★ **STAR 2**			
	★ **STAR 3**			
	★ **STAR 1**			
	★ **STAR 2**			
	★ **STAR 3**			
	★ **STAR 1**			
	★ **STAR 2**			
	★ **STAR 3**			
	★ **STAR 1**			
	★ **STAR 2**			
	★ **STAR 3**			
	★ **STAR 1**			
	★ **STAR 2**			
	★ **STAR 3**			

Preparation Exercise

Profiling the Job You Are Seeking

Dimension	STARs: Recent, Job Related, Demonstrate Mastery/ Improvement	Rating 1 = Low; 5 = High	Shining?	Best Match?
Behavioral Dimensions				
	★ STAR 1			
	★ STAR 2			
	★ STAR 3			
	★ STAR 1			
	★ STAR 2			
	★ STAR 3			
	★ STAR 1			
	★ STAR 2			
	★ STAR 3			
	★ STAR 1			
	★ STAR 2			
	★ STAR 3			
	★ STAR 1			
	★ STAR 2			
	★ STAR 3			

Profiling the Job You Are Seeking

Dimension	STARs: Recent, Job Related, Demonstrate Mastery/ Improvement	Rating 1 = Low; 5 = High	Shining?	Best Match?
Behavioral Dimensions				
	★ STAR 1			
	★ STAR 2			
	★ STAR 3			
	★ STAR 1			
	★ STAR 2			
	★ STAR 3			
	★ STAR 1			
	★ STAR 2			
	★ STAR 3			
	★ STAR 1			
	★ STAR 2			
	★ STAR 3			
	★ STAR 1			
	★ STAR 2			
	★ STAR 3			

Preparation Exercise

Profiling the Job You Are Seeking

Dimension	STARs: Recent, Job Related, Demonstrate Mastery/ Improvement	Rating 1 = Low; 5 = High	Shining?	Best Match?
Motivational Facets				
	★ STAR 1			
	★ STAR 2			
	★ STAR 3			
	★ STAR 1			
	★ STAR 2			
	★ STAR 3			
	★ STAR 1			
	★ STAR 2			
	★ STAR 3			
	★ STAR 1			
	★ STAR 2			
	★ STAR 3			
	★ STAR 1			
	★ STAR 2			
	★ STAR 3			

NOTES

CUPID'S ARROW: MATCHING YOUR DIMENSIONS TO THE JOB

7

Steps to Making a Match

What to Do If There's a Mismatch

How Important Are Dimensions You Have But Can't Use in the Job?

How to Check Your Match

CUPID'S ARROW: MATCHING YOUR DIMENSIONS TO THE JOB

Derek had been sure he wanted to go into marketing. His roommate from college, Jeff, had a marketing job, and it sounded great. Derek's vision of life in the marketing coordinator position was of day-long brainstorming sessions, planning the best strategy to market Milletech's communications technology to any industry. And who would know better? Derek had helped to design most of the technology. He'd be able to come up with a thousand ideas. And he'd have an ample staff of writers, graphics people, and event planners to execute those ideas. It hadn't occurred to Derek that he'd be the staff. So it came as something of a shock to him when just before his interview, Ellen in HR handed him the job description to look over.

Position Description

Marketing coordinator will work as a member of the marketing team to:

- Coordinate multiple (20-30) marketing activities simultaneously.
- Plan events—all aspects from inception to tracking results, sales, and budgets.
- Develop, design, and manage direct-mail campaigns.
- Coordinate telemarketing to qualify leads and generate event attendance; train telemarketers.
- Maintain extensive phone and limited face-to-face contact with clients.
- Develop territory marketing tactics.
- Maintain archives of information, such as references, competitive files, marketing materials, and proposals.
- Make presentations at regional meetings and marketing events as needed and appropriate.

Direct mail? Telemarketing? He hadn't thought about doing any of those things. He wasn't sure he knew how. And besides, he wasn't sure he wanted to know. Looking back on it, he supposed it was a good thing that he hadn't been offered the marketing job. Still, though, he was serious about making a change. He decided to take a different approach. Maybe it was a good idea to look at job descriptions first.

Milletech's venture into the business communications industry had created opportunities in a wide range of sales and marketing positions, and Derek was convinced that he could apply his technical knowledge in one of those positions. Attempting to shake off his rejection, he headed back to HR to check out the postings. How many more rejections could possibly face him?

Derek looked over the job postings and thought again, "Maybe not." He wasn't sure he knew how to do any of the jobs that were available.

He tore down the posting that looked most interesting and headed home to consider his options. ✭

Steps to Making a Match

A successful job interview matches the dimensions (knowledge/skill, behavioral, and motivational) of the applicant to the dimensions needed for job success. It is the job of both the interviewer and the job seeker to determine the extent of the match and make an appropriate decision.

An effective interviewer plans the interview around the most important dimensions. The interviewer's job is to get STARs from you on each critical dimension in order to judge the quality of the match. You provide the STARs asked for as well as additional STARs on the dimensions that you feel are most important to the job, even if the interviewer fails to ask specific questions. The number and quality of your STARs are all-important. Quality is determined by the STAR's relevance to the specific job requirements and also by its recency and how well it illustrates your mastery of the dimension.

The preparation exercise you began in chapter 6 guides you through the four steps of making a job match. These are:

1. Identify the job's dimensions.

2. Think through your STARs in each of those dimensions.

3. Rate the quality of your STARs and note "shining" STARs (best STAR for each dimension).

4. Choose your best-matched dimensions (those that are strengths for you and that are important to the job).

Taking the time to write out a brief summary of behavioral examples helps you plant them firmly in your mind so you will remember them during the interview. Don't worry about seeming stilted or rehearsed; you won't sound that way to the interviewer. The interviewer will be impressed by the smoothness of your answers. Furthermore, the interviewer will be thrilled about obtaining needed information so easily.

Writing out your STARs will also help you learn what to listen for during your interview. If you've thought about what the job entails and how your experiences qualify you to succeed in it, you'll more clearly understand what an interviewer is looking for from specific questions. For example, perhaps your research shows that the job requires decisiveness in the form of quick responses to competitive marketing initiatives. If the competition offers a sale price or promotion in one part of the country, the person in the job must quickly decide how to respond.

Armed with this information, you will be prepared when your interviewer asks about decisions you have made and will know to describe how rapidly you have been able to come to high-quality decisions.

Once you have evaluated your STARs, you can begin to plan the STARs you want to be sure to discuss in your interview. To do this, think about the dimensions that are most important to success in the job you want. The dimensions that are most important and for which you have the highest rated STAR examples are your best-matched dimensions.

The dimensions that are most important and for which you have the highest rated STAR examples are your best-matched dimensions.

☆ ☆ ☆ ☆ ☆ ☆

For all his dedication to his work, Derek loved coming home at the end of a day. The kids were often already in bed, but on Friday evenings they stayed up late and greeted him with kisses as he came through the front door. It was what he'd always imagined coming home to mean. He wished he'd gotten that greeting tonight, those little arms wrapped tightly around him. But Elaine had taken Kevin and Julie to visit her sister on the coast.

Derek hit the speed dial to order a pizza and unpacked his briefcase. He took a second look at the job description he'd brought home. ☆

Position Description

Account executive will work as a member of the sales team to:

- Grow sales revenue by representing Milletech Industries in the marketplace.
- Develop and execute strategic sales plans that promote acquisition of clients.
- After one year, maintain a list of 40 key accounts (clients and prospects) through continuously qualifying leads and making strategic business decisions about which accounts to pursue.
- Develop new business opportunities with targeted key prospects.
- Negotiate fees with high-level executives.
- Seek opportunities for additional product and service expansion with existing clients.
- Interact with high-level executives to determine the best communications solutions for their organizations.
- Develop detailed technical proposals as part of the sales process.
- Provide regular, timely information to Milletech about sales and customer service activities, sales forecasts, wins/losses, etc.

Derek knew he could represent Milletech in the marketplace. Who better than one of the engineers who had designed the technology they were famous for? And he could certainly work with people to design solutions. And write impressive proposals. He was used to reporting information back to the company. He was sure he could do it—everything except the actual selling part. And the planning involved to get new accounts. So where did that leave him?

The way Derek figured it, the most important dimensions for the account executive job were:

1. Sales ability
2. Customer orientation
3. (Sales) Planning and organizing
4. Decision making (about which clients to pursue)

Later, as he wolfed down the last slice of sausage and mushroom pizza, Derek considered his competence in those areas. He sort of had sales ability: He had often convinced people to adopt his point of view. And he did a decent job of being customer focused—when his customers weren't complete morons. "Hmm," he muttered, "note to self: That one needs work." He knew he had skill in planning and organizing, though he didn't know much about sales planning.

Derek wasn't sure—maybe it was just his heartburn kicking in—but he had a good feeling about this. He could see himself as a salesman. An account executive. It had a nice ring to it. He grabbed some paper from his briefcase and began to compare his dimensions to those required in the sales job.

Part of Derek's list looked like pages 106 and 107. ✯

Profiling the Job You Are Seeking

Dimension	STARs: Recent, Job Related, Demonstrate Mastery/ Improvement	Rating 1 = Low; 5 = High	Shining?	Best Match?
Behavioral Dimensions				
Sales Ability: Using appropriate interpersonal styles and communication methods to gain acceptance of an idea, plan, service, or product from prospects and clients.	★ **STAR 1** *Multiple groups were working on different aspects of a complex project. My team, ComSystems, took the lead. In making the presentation to management, I had to incorporate information from all the groups. I used the information to make charts and displays. They were really useful to the managers, who needed to process the information. The managers gave us the go-ahead.*	3		
	★ **STAR 2** *A project that was assigned to navigation systems really should have been handled by my team. I assembled information about similar projects we'd handled before and submitted a lengthy memo to support our case. Management reassigned the project.*	2		
	★ **STAR 3**			
Customer Orientation: Effectively meeting customer needs; building productive customer relationships; taking responsibility for customer satisfaction.	★ **STAR 1** *With the communications system for the X-46, the ranking officers wanted things that were just impossible. I listened to their requests, and I tried to cover everything I could, but there were some things that I just couldn't deliver. I had to explain things over and over, but they ended up being pretty satisfied.*	2		
	★ **STAR 2**			
	★ **STAR 3**			

Preparation Exercise

Profiling the Job You Are Seeking

Dimension	STARs: Recent, Job Related, Demonstrate Mastery/ Improvement	Rating 1 = Low; 5 = High	Shining?	Best Match?
Behavioral Dimensions				
Planning and Organizing: Establishing a course of action for self and others to accomplish a specific goal; planning proper assignments of personnel and appropriate allocation of resources.	★ **STAR 1** *On the X-46 project, I used a Gantt chart to map out the personnel and resources we were using, as well as the timeline we'd need to follow. I posted the chart outside my office. It was so helpful to me in keeping up with the details of the project that I've managed all my projects since then in the same way. I've been on time and close to budget all year.*	4		
	★ **STAR 2** *Three years ago I was in charge of planning the company picnic. I used a survey to determine what kind of activities people would like. I kept track of all the arrangements using a "tickler" file that I checked daily. By treating the picnic like any other major project, I was able to organize it so that it came off without a hitch. Except it rained.*	2		
	★ **STAR 3** *A while back, I was asked to chair a fundraiser for the alumni society of my fraternity. I had never done anything like that, so I spent a lot of time with past chairmen to find out what was involved and drew up a plan. Because I took the time to write things out, it was easy to keep up with all the details. Also, I had something concrete to hand off to the next chairman. My event had a record number of donations, largely because I was so thorough in contacting every possible contributor.*	3		

We show Derek's STARs in detail to demonstrate how he thought them through. It's usually not necessary to write such a complete description. A few words or notes will do; as long as you understand them, they don't have to be clear to anyone else.

Evaluating his work, Derek recognized some flaws in his examples. For one thing, he didn't have many. And they weren't as recent as he would have liked. Most of the projects he'd mentioned were more than a year old. He'd once been meticulous about tracking his own performance, but he'd fallen out of the habit.

Most of Derek's examples were related to his job as an engineer and a design team leader; because they didn't relate directly to the sales job, they weren't truly "job related." Derek began to think that even "planning and organizing," a dimension he considered to be among his strengths, might be a challenge for him in a sales role. His STARs weren't bad; the outputs were just very different from those that would be required in sales. While Derek could "stretch" some of his experiences to relate them to sales, he could clearly see there was a lot to learn. The AE job wasn't what he'd call a perfect match.

★ ★ ★ ★ ★ ★

Milletech had never really had salespeople. The company had never needed them because it had only one customer—the government. Milletech had people called relationship managers who performed the sales function. The relationship managers and assigned senior executives maintained business relationships with purchasers in the military, and as long as those relationships existed, requests for proposals came in and designs went out. The military needed technology, and Milletech supplied it. Derek had always liked the way the business was run. It meant that he could spend a lot of time talking and building friendships with the customers who used his designs in the field.

Occasionally, Derek would accompany one of the relationship managers to a meeting and "talk up" his design work. Those presentations were simple to plan—it was easy to guess who

Milletech's competitors would be, and Derek knew the strengths and weaknesses of all of them. Besides, the relationship managers did most of the "schmoozing"; all Derek had to do was talk about his project, and he could do that endlessly. He thought that selling telecommunications products to businesses would be different, but he wasn't sure how.

He considered calling the new vice president, Jill Zucker. She was leading the new venture, "Mille-Cel." (Most of Derek's colleagues referred to it as "Mille-Sell.") The business communications division was capturing everyone's attention, and Jill Zucker seemed to be everywhere. Derek thought about what he would ask Jill and how he could phrase his request so it wouldn't sound as if he were begging for a job. If he worded his message carefully, he could send it on e-mail. Derek thought that one-way communication was always a smart choice.

What should he ask, though, without sounding unprofessional? He tore off a clean sheet of paper and began making some notes.

Sales ability
I've been on sales calls, but I've never:
- Taken a lead role
- Met a telecommunications customer

Customer orientation
I've dealt with customers, but I've never:
- Been responsible for their overall satisfaction

(Sales) Planning and organizing
I'm great at managing my time and keeping up with several projects, but I've never:
- Applied that to any kind of selling

Decision making (about which clients to pursue)
As a leader, I'm a pretty good decision maker, but I've never:
- Applied that to any kind of selling

Derek decided that he needed to talk to someone about all his "but I've never . . ." statements. How could he gain experience in those things? He doubted that in the middle of creating a huge corporate venture, Jill would be eager to spend time tutoring him. Still, he wanted to let her know that he was interested in sales.

Waiting for an idea to come, Derek pulled the laptop from his briefcase. As the computer booted up, he heard the familiar "ding" that indicated he had an e-mail message. In fact, he had several. Still contemplating how to make a move for a sales position, he started to read his mail. He deleted the first one. Nothing that was sent out to the whole company was ever worth reading. "Junk," he pronounced. He'd almost deleted the second one, when he noticed whom it was from. He double-clicked to open it.

```
To:   All Associates
From: Jill Zucker
Re:   AE Training—Next Two Weeks

In order to conduct Mille-Cel
technical and sales training for
account executives, we have
reserved Conference Rooms A & B
for the next two weeks, beginning
Monday. In addition, Meeting
Rooms 1 to 5 on the second floor
will be unavailable for use by
associates outside the sales and
marketing group. We apologize for
any inconvenience this may cause.
```

"Whoa—not junk. AE training." Derek had the beginning of an idea. All the people he'd want to talk to would be assembled in one place for the next two weeks. But he still had to figure out what to say.

☆ ☆ ☆ ☆ ☆ ☆

"Mr. Johnson, I don't think we've been formally introduced. I'm Derek Robertson."

Bill Johnson had the grip of an ex-college football player. Big 10. He was the kind of guy who was at once instantly likable, but somehow reserved. Speaking with him, Derek had the feeling that Bill was holding something back.

It didn't take long to figure out what that was. "It's a great idea," Bill said, pausing before he continued, "but I'm going to have to run it by Jill Zucker. She's been under tremendous stress developing this training. And there isn't a minute to spare in the schedule."

"I'm not suggesting any changes to the schedule. I just want to make myself available as a coach if anyone needs more detail or background on communication systems." Derek wanted this to work out; it would be a great "in" for him, and he knew he could do it. And the more people he met in Sales and Marketing, the better.

Bill nodded. "Let me see what I can do. You'd definitely be a valuable resource for these new AEs. And, who knows, they might be able to teach you a thing or two."

"That's the idea," Derek laughed. That was the whole idea.

The two exchanged another firm handshake and agreed to keep in touch.

"OK," thought Derek. "That's part one of the plan. If I can position myself as a technical resource for the sales force, I might be able to go on some sales calls. Now, for part two."

He headed toward the office of one of his team members. Michelle was a great talker, and he hadn't spoken with her recently because she'd just returned from vacation. He was sure she would have a million stories to tell and be in just the right frame of mind to listen to his proposition.

Derek and Michelle spent a few minutes catching up, but as she began to tell him about her adventure with an out-of-control moped, he cut her off. "Listen, Michelle, there's something I've been wanting to talk to you about. You've always done a great job presenting our team's designs. I mean, you have the strongest communication skills of anyone on our team. But, with all the changes going on around here . . ."

"Wait a minute," Michelle interrupted. "You're not firing me, are you? You can't fire someone the day they get back from vacation. There's some kind of rule about that."

"I'm definitely not firing you. Besides, they'd send a vice president to do that."

"Funny. Go on, then," said Michelle.

"I'd like to try my hand at making a few presentations. I was hoping you'd help me out—give me some advice. You know."

"Once I teach you everything, then are you going to fire me?" asked Michelle.

"I hadn't thought about that." Derek deadpanned his response, but only for a second, and broke into a grin. His plans were coming together. He was going to make himself into an account executive. ★

What to Do If There's a Mismatch

You might find that you lack STARs in some of the most important dimensions. If you realize that you might not be the best match for a job, you can choose among four options:

- Go to the interview and hope that the interviewer isn't perceptive enough to see the gaps between the profiles.

- Use the interview to emphasize the skills you have that compensate for the skills you lack. For example, if you lack knowledge in a certain area but can demonstrate a high ability to learn and the motivation to do so, the interviewer will view these strengths as a way of overcoming the mismatch.

  In other situations you'll be able to demonstrate how you can work around a particular area. For example, a manager who struggles with written communication might be able to clearly explain his ideas orally and delegate the task of writing to a subordinate.

  The chart on page 113 can help you understand the idea of compensating dimensions. Read these examples and think about how they might help you match your target job.

- Back out of the interview to win time to develop your strengths (STARs) in the most important dimensions for the job. This is what Derek did.

- Decide that the job isn't appropriate for you and back out of the interview process entirely. It is often better to drop out of the selection process when you know that you and the position aren't a good match than it is to suffer the ego-deflating results of a rejection. If you have already scheduled an interview, you might consider using that time as a way of finding out about other jobs in the organization that would be a better fit for you. You might even start off the interview by summarizing your understanding of the dimensions required in the job and offering your evaluation of how you stack up against those dimensions. Then you can say that while you are not a perfect match for the position, you have a number of strengths to offer the organization and ask if there are other jobs for which you are better suited.

If you lack STARs in . . .	You may compensate with strong STARs in . . .
Technical Knowledge	Initiative; Ability to Learn
Project Management	Delegation
Impact	Follow-through
Written Communication	Delegation/Oral Communication
Sales Ability	Persuasiveness; Ability to Learn
Creativity	Empowerment/Management Control

How Important Are Dimensions You Have But Can't Use in the Job?

If you're great at math, but applying for a job that doesn't involve numbers, how important is that mathematical ability? Extra dimensions generally won't help you get a job, but they won't hurt either. In fact, they make you stand out from other applicants or identify you as well rounded. The larger issue is your happiness. Should you consider a job that doesn't use all your skills? Yes! If you're skilled in a dimension that you don't use on the job, you might look for another outlet—perhaps freelance work if you're a talented writer or a position on the finance committee of a volunteer organization if you have a mind for numbers.

Accepting a position in which you won't be using all your strengths and talents is a tough decision. You might decide to take the job in the hope that it will lead to a promotion or transfer that will involve more of your skills. Or you might find yourself using your dimensions in a new way. For example, many law school graduates find out that their law degrees aren't nearly as valuable as they'd hoped when they are competing against other law school grads for jobs in law firms. But many of those same people discover that their degrees are extremely valuable in other fields, such as human resources or compensation consulting, where the degree differentiates them from their peers.

Remember, the perfect job exists only in a perfect world. Few jobs will use all your skills and talents. Your satisfaction and, ultimately, your feeling of fulfillment will come from all aspects of your life, personal and professional.

How to Check Your Match

Go back to the preparation exercise, "Profiling the Job You Are Seeking," on page 94 and fill in the rest of the columns. For example, if you filled in "Can use spreadsheet software" as the first knowledge/skill dimension, write up to three STAR examples of situations in which you've applied that skill. Three good STARs are usually enough to prove your strength in a dimension.

When writing your STARs, remember to review the STARs you wrote in chapters 2 through 5. Many of those will be applicable to the dimensions you've listed.

Don't feel constrained by the STARs you've thought of up until now. If you can come up with additional STARs or STARs more related to your target job, do so. Don't worry if you don't have three or more complete STARs for each dimension. In fact, you might not have any for some dimensions. Most candidates do have gaps. Remember to think "outside the box" for STARs and include things you've learned and done outside the classroom or workplace.

The best STARs are both recent and job related. For example, your strongest STARs related to spreadsheet software will deal with times when you used these programs to do tasks similar to those in your target job. In the space provided on pages 94-97, rate each STAR from 1 to 5 on its job relatedness, its quality, and its recency. A "5" means that the STAR deals with a situation common to the target job, the skill application or behavior occurred in the last year or two, the issues involved were substantive, and your skill or behavior meant something to the organization. When rating a STAR for some facet of motivational fit, consider how recent it is, its job relatedness, and whether it demonstrates its importance to your performance. Make a check mark to note your strongest, or "shining," STAR for each dimension. This is the STAR you should bring out first when your interviewer covers that subject area.

Finally, decide which three dimensions will be your "best-matched" dimensions—those that are most important for the job you want and for which you have the strongest STARs. These are the dimensions you want to bring out early in your interview. They might be knowledge/skill, behavioral, or motivational dimensions. Most often they are behavioral dimensions. Remind yourself to discuss them in your interviews by checking the far right column.

Preparation Exercise

How to Check Your Match

Because these best-matched dimensions are your strongest selling points, it is important that no matter what, you make the interviewer aware of them. If you aren't able to cover them during the interview, bring them up at the end of the interview when most interviewers will give you an opportunity to ask questions. You should not leave the interview without covering these dimensions. Chapter 8 gives you some tips on covering these dimensions from the very beginning of your interview.

Carefully consider your answers as you complete the exercise, "Profiling the Job You Are Seeking." The purpose of this exercise is to provide you with a realistic picture of how closely your dimension profile matches that of your target job. Be truthful with yourself–it's your life, and who would you be fooling anyway?

For all jobs you are seeking, make up a chart similar to the one shown on pages 94-97. Each time you complete a chart, your task will be easier, and you'll gain familiarity with dimensions and STARs. Also, you will usually find an overlap among dimensions for the positions you are seeking.

NOTES

SO, TELL ME ABOUT YOURSELF: OPENING THE INTERVIEW

8

SO, TELL ME ABOUT YOURSELF: OPENING THE INTERVIEW

Derek squirmed in his seat. The administrative assistant had said that Ms. Zucker would join him in a moment. Derek hoped he could collect his thoughts and calm his stomach before his interviewer walked into the room. It had been painful to be rejected for the marketing coordinator position, and here he was setting himself up for it again.

But this time, he told himself, was different. He'd worked hard to make contacts within the sales force. A number of the account executives had come to him with technical questions, and he'd even had the chance to go on a few sales calls as a technical advisor. Between that experience and the coaching he'd gotten from Michelle on his presentation skills, Derek felt much more prepared in going after this job.

This morning he'd almost lost his nerve and backed out of the interview entirely. He'd called Jill Zucker to cancel, but hung up when he got her voice mail. He wasn't sure if he could handle the rejection that might come, but on the other hand, he was determined to show his job fit. He was confident he could sell himself.

"Hi, Derek. Sorry you had to wait." Jill Zucker, Milletech's newest vice president, had already acquired that slightly out-of-breath tone that was common to so many people across the company. It was a company that had a reputation for attracting workaholics—creative, dedicated, energetic people who seemed lost when they couldn't be at the office. Derek typed Jill as one of those people.

Jill had the manner of a person struggling for focus. She carried a large planner, thick with business cards and notes, that revealed a failed effort at organization.

"Now, let's see . . . I've got your resume right here." She thumbed through several sections of the organizer before she put a hand on it.

"I guess I still have quite a way to go toward becoming 'paperless,'" Jill joked as she thumbed through her organizer once again, apparently looking for her notes.

She began, "First of all, as I'm sure you know, your boss has told me some terrific things about you, Derek. I'm excited to hear about what you think you can bring to the sales team."

"Thanks," replied Derek, wondering what Mr. Justy had said. More important, he wondered what he was supposed to say. That wasn't really a question, was it?

"Why don't we talk about some of the projects that you've worked on here at Milletech. I'd like to learn more about what your role here has been."

Derek's response was tentative: "What exactly would you like to know?" He felt like the interview was already moving in the wrong direction—away from sales—but he didn't know what to say to get things back on track.

He slumped deeper into his chair. ✯

Getting Started

Getting started in an interview often can be awkward. Many interviewers begin with a very general question or remark such as, "So, tell me about yourself." The work you've done identifying your dimensions and matching them to the job can be very useful to you in planning your response. For example, you might say:

"In preparation for this job interview, I was thinking about what I could say about myself. I guess you'd like to know about some of the things I've done in the areas of leadership, planning, and public opinion polling. Is that correct, or did I miss something? Then which is most important? I'll start there."

A well-trained interviewer will begin with a specific question, often one designed to put you at ease by noting a positive feature of your background. For example, an interviewer might say:

"I've been anxious to meet you. I've looked over your resume and was impressed by . . . " or:

"I've been looking forward to talking with you. I noted in your resume that you are a math major, but you've also taken a number of courses in welding. I'd like to hear how that came about."

It is usually acceptable for you to wait until the interviewer begins the conversation. The interviewer might be getting papers in order or collecting thoughts. It's probably best for you not to interrupt that process.

Sometimes, however, a few minutes of silence will hang heavy, and you'll need to start the conversation. There are two good ways to get the ball rolling. One is to make a positive comment about the organization and how you see yourself contributing to it. You might say:

"I'm happy to have this chance to talk to you. Your company has a wonderful reputation in our town, and I am familiar with some of the marketing work your department has turned out."

A second way to begin the conversation is to ask a question, such as one of the following:

"Could you tell me some more about the job? I'm interested in hearing about the kind of work I might be doing."

"I was wondering what issues are driving the need to create this job?"

"I understand you have several jobs open. What is causing the growth in the number of positions available?"

Asking questions early in the interview helps you determine the job dimensions most important to your interviewer. Such questions will facilitate your conversation and define the business elements central to your discussion.

> *Asking questions early in the interview helps you determine the job dimensions most important to your interviewer.*

Keep in mind, however, that the beginning of the interview is not the time to ask questions about such areas as compensation and benefits. It is appropriate to ask about specific job duties and motivational facets of job and organizational fit, such as whether you would be working in a team. This information helps you judge which of your STARs to discuss as the interview moves along.

A third way to begin the conversation is to speak to your interviewer's interests. Look around the office. Are there numerous group photos? You might ask whether they are pictures of teams he or she has been on. This would be a great way to launch a discussion of your experience in working in teams.

Here are some tips from DDI's human resource experts on opening an interview:

Regarding Small Talk and Talking Sports, Etc.
Making light conversation about the weather or sports is not a "bad" thing to do, but such conversations rarely help you feel more at ease because they're not part of the "real" interview. Moreover, they are a waste of limited, valuable time. You usually have less than an hour to convey to the interviewer your most positive qualities. Our experts advise that you don't waste a minute of that opportunity, especially when your comments might risk offending a fan of your team's rival. Of course, if your interviewer attempts to put you at ease with such a conversation, you should participate fully.

Checking Out What You Know About the Organization and Clearing the Way for Your STARs
If you are in your second or third interview for a position, you might want to begin with a summary of your understanding of the job and its responsibilities. Sometimes you can do this on a first interview if you have done a lot of homework on the company and job or if you

have an internal coach who has helped you gather information about the position.

This summary is an important check on your understanding. The interviewer can easily correct any misunderstandings you might have about the job or organization. Interviewers usually don't mind doing that and don't consider it a negative that you might have misunderstood some information. The fact that you've prepared and spent time thinking about the job can only be viewed as a positive. And the clarification the interviewer provides will help you know what's most important to discuss.

You can take the summary a step further and share your guesses at the most important dimensions. After the interviewer affirms their importance or corrects your perceptions, ask for more information. For example, you might ask how the organization identifies and measures these skills in its employees over time.

Use Your Best-Matched Dimensions and Shining STARs

Interviewers often make decisions about candidates in the first few minutes of the interview, and those early decisions affect how subsequent interview data are interpreted. Thus, if the interviewer gives you a chance, mention your best-matched dimensions early in the interview and illustrate each with a shining STAR.

If you have determined (in an earlier interview or discussion) that a particular dimension is important or if you have confirmed a particular business need, the opening of the interview is a wonderful opportunity to use a shining STAR to assert your strength in the dimension. You might say something like:

"I'm pleased to hear that you take a consultative approach to sales. It fits right into my background. At RST Company, I . . ." or:

"Your expansion plans certainly are aggressive, particularly in the Far East. I spent my high school years in Jakarta and speak Bahasa."

Some Things to Watch For

Is the interviewer following a guide? If so, expect the interviewer to control the interview from beginning to end. If the interviewer does not have a guide or seems ill prepared, you have a much better chance to guide the interview yourself.

What to Call the Interviewer

You can never go wrong by calling the interviewer "Ms." or "Mr." Use the person's first name only if he or she suggests it. After the protocol is settled, use the interviewer's name as often as possible during the interview.

Preparation Exercise

Practice Your Openers

How could Derek have managed this exchange more effectively? Below and on the next page are Jill's "openers" and some hints that will help you develop responses more effective than Derek's. Taking the time to write out how you would respond will help you get over your jitters. Being prepared will build your confidence and improve the impact you make. Write what you would say in the space provided.

"Hi, Derek. Sorry you had to wait."

Hint: After you have offered a relaxed, confident handshake, it's never wrong to compliment the organization or the interviewer, if you have the facts to do it. An expression of your positive expectations for the interview, based on your research or on your past interviews, sets a good tone.

"Now let's see . . . I've got your resume right here."

Hint: If you faxed your resume to your interviewer, you might want to offer a clean copy. Always have a copy of your resume ready in case the interviewer can't find it. Also, this might be a good time to offer additional materials you were asked to bring, such as samples of your work.

Practice Your Openers

"First of all, as I'm sure you know, your boss has told me some terrific things about you, Derek. I'm excited to hear about what you think you can bring to the sales team."

Hint: Express your appreciation for the recommendation. Answer with a statement about your best-matched dimensions and how they have impressed people (such as your bosses) in the past. Keep the statement brief (no need for a STAR at this point) and allow the interviewer to guide the conversation.

"Why don't we talk about some of the projects that you've worked on here at Milletech. I'd like to learn more about what your role here has been."

Hint: Be sure to mention projects that were similar to those you'd be doing in the new job or that required skill in one of the target job's key dimensions.

A DAY IN THE LIFE: BEHAVIORAL SIMULATIONS AND TESTS

9

Behavioral Simulations

Paper-and-Pencil Tests

Psychologists–What They Ask and How to Answer

A DAY IN THE LIFE: BEHAVIORAL SIMULATIONS AND TESTS

"They're torturing me," Sara declared. "It's the only possible explanation." Sara was not amused. The message on her answering machine from Ingrid Zwerner's office was a request that she return to ZIPR headquarters to participate in a "behavioral simulation." Hadn't she been told that she wasn't going to get the junior assistant account representative job? And what was a behavioral simulation anyway?

"Behavioral simulation. Isn't that rats running through mazes or something?" Dan clearly was amused.

"I'm not doing it. I'm not." She put on her difficult-middle-child face, which usually meant she wasn't going to budge.

"Oh, come on. You can't quit now. You're a role model for slackers like me."

The idea of being a role model was Sara's soft spot. While she enjoyed neither poverty nor desperation, she did feel a sense of moral superiority as a result of her job search. While Dan, currently nursing his creative ambitions as

a bookstore clerk, was provided with a new car (his second) and rent-free living by his parents, Sara had always patched together part-time jobs and freelance work to meet her expenses. She did her best to instill guilt in Dan so he'd pick up the tab for their outings; it wasn't really his money, after all. And, she'd point out, all her suffering would be rewarded someday (Sara believed the universe to be just), and she would gladly repay him. In the meantime she earned her keep by entertaining her friend with horror stories from her job hunt.

Dan was thinking about what a great story she would have afterward. It would be up there with the ones about the CEO who made her read his self-published autobiography and the vice president who kept her waiting for three hours. More than that, he knew she wanted the job.

"All right, you can sit here while I call them back, if you swear that you'll be quiet." Sara picked up the phone and began dialing the number she had committed to memory.

Ingrid's assistant answered in a tone that smacked of efficiency. Sara admired that. In preparation for her career as an executive, she was training herself to answer the phone by stating her name, rather than with a tentative "hello."

"You know, I'm not sure I know what a behavioral simulation is," Sara said into the phone after a few seconds of pleasantries. Dan watched her frown and furrowed brow grow into a smile.

The reply Sara received boiled down to, "Come in and pretend that you've got the job." In that case, she decided, how bad could it be?

It was, after all, ***the*** job. Sara was willing to do more than pretend she had it. ✯

Behavioral Simulations

Most organizations gather information from more than just interviews to make hiring or promotion decisions. The most common sources are behavioral simulations, paper-and-pencil tests, and the insights of trained psychologists.

Behavioral simulations are situations in which you are asked to demonstrate dimensions. For example, if you are applying for a sales position, you might receive information about a hypothetical product and a particular customer and be asked to prepare for a sales call with that customer. You then conduct the sales call with a representative of the company, who plays the role of the customer. Usually, a second company representative observes your performance and notes strengths and weaknesses in particular dimensions.

In another type of behavioral simulation, you receive items similar to what would be found in the in-basket of a person who holds a position similar to the one you are seeking. You are told to go through the items just as you would in real life. Beginning below is an excerpt from the instructions for an exercise appropriate for candidates for management positions.

Directions for In-Basket Simulation

Overview:

For the next few hours you will assume the role of Max Johnson, branch manager of Continental Diversified Containers (CDC), a manufacturer of glass bottles and bottling equipment with home offices in Saddlewood, Connecticut. The date is Saturday, February 2.

You are married to Pat Johnson and have two children, John, 20, and Mary, 18. You are 41 years of age and hold a bachelor of science degree from Gamma College. You have worked 14 years for CDC, beginning as a salesperson and working your way up to national account executive. Prior to coming to CDC, you served in the armed services and worked two years as a sales representative for Marco Plastics.

Directions for In-Basket Simulation

You just finished training your replacement and were looking forward to attending the "Fundamentals of Management" course offered by the corporation to prepare you for an expected branch managership in the eastern region. This is an intensive, week-long training program during which no outside contacts are allowed. Then, on Wednesday, January 30, Warren Watkins, midwest regional sales manager, offered you the position of manager of the Nottingham branch, reporting to him. The position suddenly became vacant when Jerry Hartwig, the manager of Nottingham, suffered a heart attack last week while on a camping trip with his family. He was rushed to the hospital by life-flight helicopter but died on Monday morning, January 28.

Watkins was able to provide information about the Nottingham branch.

Your Task:

It is now Saturday, February 2, 1 p.m. You are in your new office and have a few hours to take care of the items in Hartwig's in-basket before you continue on to the training program. Everyone is out of the office and the switchboard is closed, so you can't make any calls. You must work alone and have access only to the materials that your assistant has left for you. You want to do well and make a good impression on Watkins. It is important that you let your subordinates know exactly what you plan to do with each item in the in-basket, so everything you do or plan to do should be in writing. In going through the items, you can write notes, memos, and letters; plan meetings; and make decisions. You should also plan all phone calls you intend to make regarding any of the items when you officially start on the job. You may write directly on the item or use the supply of stationery provided. When using the stationery, clip any notes or letters you write to the related item.

Remember:

It is Saturday, February 2, 1 p.m. You will not report to work officially until Monday, February 11, 8:30 a.m., and you will not be able to phone anyone until then.

By looking at your actions in simulations, the organization is able to observe and evaluate your decision-making, planning, delegation, problem-solving, and other skills.

Another common simulation asks you to analyze complicated data, prepare a written presentation, and then make an oral presentation of your recommendations based on the data.

Assessment simulations are evaluated by a trained individual within the organization or by a specialist from outside the organization. These observers might be present for the simulation or might review your performance on videotape.

Simulations are particularly useful when you have little direct experience in a comparable position. If you've never held a sales job, you might have difficulty discussing STAR examples that demonstrate sales ability. A solid performance in a simulation, along with relevant STARs (such as examples of times when you've had to sell an idea or solicit funds), gives you credibility even if you're inexperienced.

Behavioral simulations are also excellent adjuncts to interviews because they offer the interviewer a check on your skill level and thus help measure the accuracy of your answers in the interview. In a simulation you have the opportunity to show the interviewer what you can do and to reinforce points you've made during interviews. You'll win points for credibility if you can demonstrate the skills you've claimed to have.

Even weaknesses in a simulation performance will not necessarily work against you if you have realistically discussed your dimension profile. The most important thing to remember is that the answers you offer in an interview must be consistent with your performance in a simulation. It's another reason why lying in an interview doesn't work.

There is no way of "beating" a well-conducted behavioral simulation. The worst thing you can do is to try to be someone you are not. Our advice is to be yourself and handle the simulation situation as you would handle a real-life situation. If, after you finish a simulation, you are asked to evaluate your performance, try to discuss your performance objectively. Trying to put a positive "spin" on your mistakes isn't nearly as effective as simply identifying a mistake and moving on. Defensiveness will not impress your evaluator. Consider the following two responses to a self-evaluation question:

Candidate A: I think I did a good job of solving the problem. As the customer, you didn't seem to appreciate my sense of humor, but making light of a bad situation usually works

for me. I'm sure that in a real situation, I would have been able to judge the person's reaction.

Candidate B: I'm pleased with the way I was able to solve your problem. I was able to get you the help that you needed. However, I think that I misjudged the situation when I tried to make a joke. You were still very frustrated. Later, after the matter was resolved to your satisfaction, might have been a better time to laugh about the situation.

Simulations allow you to demonstrate the range of skills associated with successful job performance.

The candidates mention similar experiences, but their comments differ in several important ways. Each begins with a positive statement about how he or she performed in the simulation. Candidate A, however, seems to question the validity of the simulation, while justifying a mistake. Candidate B, on the other hand, identifies the mistake, explains why it was a mistake, and describes a better way to handle the situation. Which candidate would you rather work with?

It's important that you take simulations seriously. If you are given material to prepare at home, spend as much time with it as possible, within the directions provided. Approach simulations as you would your first day on the new job. Although you might feel anxious, you should also be making a good impression by working to your fullest potential.

Participating in a simulation might require some suspension of belief on your part. If you "go along," you will probably perform better than someone who takes the exercise less seriously. Simulations aren't meant to replicate all the characteristics of a typical workday—you'll probably never face a day in which you have to tackle so many problems. Simulations allow you to demonstrate the range of skills associated with successful job performance.

Poor Behavioral Simulations

Not all behavioral simulations are created equal. A well-conceived and administered simulation provides you with all the data you need to show your strengths in the dimensions under consideration. Unfortunately, some interviewers provide too little data about a simulation, which can cause them to form a wrong impression about your skills.

For example, an interviewer might toss you a cup or a paper clip and say, "Sell that to me." This simulation emphasizes quick thinking and creativity, rather than true sales ability. In this situation it is possible that an interviewer will form a negative impression about you when you would be perfectly capable in a more typical sales situation in which you're fully informed about the product and the customer and have had time to prepare.

If you face such a poor simulation, you should ask questions to set up the situation before leaping into it. You might ask questions such as, "First, would you mind telling me something about the customer? Can you give me information about the features of the product relative to its competition?" These kinds of questions impress an interviewer and help assure your best performance in the simulation.

Pencil-and-Paper Tests

We've all had tests at school. We know what they are used for, and we know whether we're good at taking them.

If an organization is using paper-and-pencil tests to supplement the information they collect in interviews, the test is probably not optional. Equal Employment Opportunity Commission regulations prohibit administering a test to only some of the people applying for the same job. In other words, if you refuse to take a test, the organization would be obliged to knock you out of the selection process.

There is a lot of debate about the merit of using tests in a selection system. Organizations administer tests for some good reasons, such as measuring critical thinking or evaluating clerical skills. There are some dangers too, such as using tests that tend to put minority applicants at a disadvantage.

Again, our best advice is to be yourself: Don't try to fake the test. Many tests contain "fakability" scales, which can trip up even the smoothest liar. You risk more damage to your chances for a position by being labeled as untruthful than by receiving a low score on a test that is only one part of the selection process.

Honesty tests often are used by organizations that are hiring or promoting people who will deal with money or confidential information. When properly validated and used, these tests are quite accurate and are designed to detect "faking."

Psychologists–What They Ask and How to Answer

Some companies might want to send you to an outside psychologist for an opinion on how well you would fit into the position or organization. Generally, a psychologist will administer a short battery of tests and conduct an interview.

The tests and interviews administered by psychologists are significantly different from those used by human resource associates within a company. They focus more on underlying personality traits that might affect your on-the-job performance than on your knowledge/skills and behaviors, and you can expect that your answers will be more deeply analyzed.

Organizations usually add psychologists to their interview teams to get unique insights into individuals and particularly to explore certain facets of motivational fit. The psychologist does not usually have the final say in a hiring decision. He or she simply provides organizational interviewers with additional information to consider in making a decision.

Sara Tecktip's name was last on the list. Ingrid Zwerner had not recommended her for the junior assistant account executive position, but Dana, Ingrid's assistant, had included her in the pool.

"I decided that her writing samples justified a second look." Dana told Ms. Zwerner in an assertive tone that belied her fear of her boss' temper. "I know that your interview with her didn't go well, but she really aced the behavioral simulation we gave her. The results show her to be highly creative, very good in presenting and defending new ideas, and a team player."

Ingrid looked nonplused. "She still doesn't have the polish to deal with clients. But if I remember correctly, she made a good impression, and her writing samples were strong."

Dana looked up, about to speak again.

Ingrid knew what was coming. Dana was going to ask her to give Sara another interview. Ingrid cut off her assistant before she could utter a word.

"Dana, I don't have time to give everyone who screws up a second chance. I'm convinced that she's not ready to work with clients, and that's the end of the discussion. Now, if there's some other position open for her and you really think she has what it takes, go ahead and move her along in the selection process. Maybe you could set up something with Peter in the creative group."

Dana nodded and took notes.

Uncharacteristically, Ingrid smiled. "Perhaps she'd be interested in your position."

Dana managed to croak out a barely audible, "Excuse me?" as her eyes widened.

"I mean, when I promote you. That way, I could give Sara a little coaching on her presentation skills—mentor her a bit."

"Promote?" Dana had started to think she'd never hear the word. She went through the motions of making a note of what her boss had said, but was sure she'd never forget it. "Thanks, boss. Great idea." ★

IF YOU WERE A TREE, WHAT KIND OF TREE WOULD YOU BE: COPING WITH DIFFICULT INTERVIEWS

10

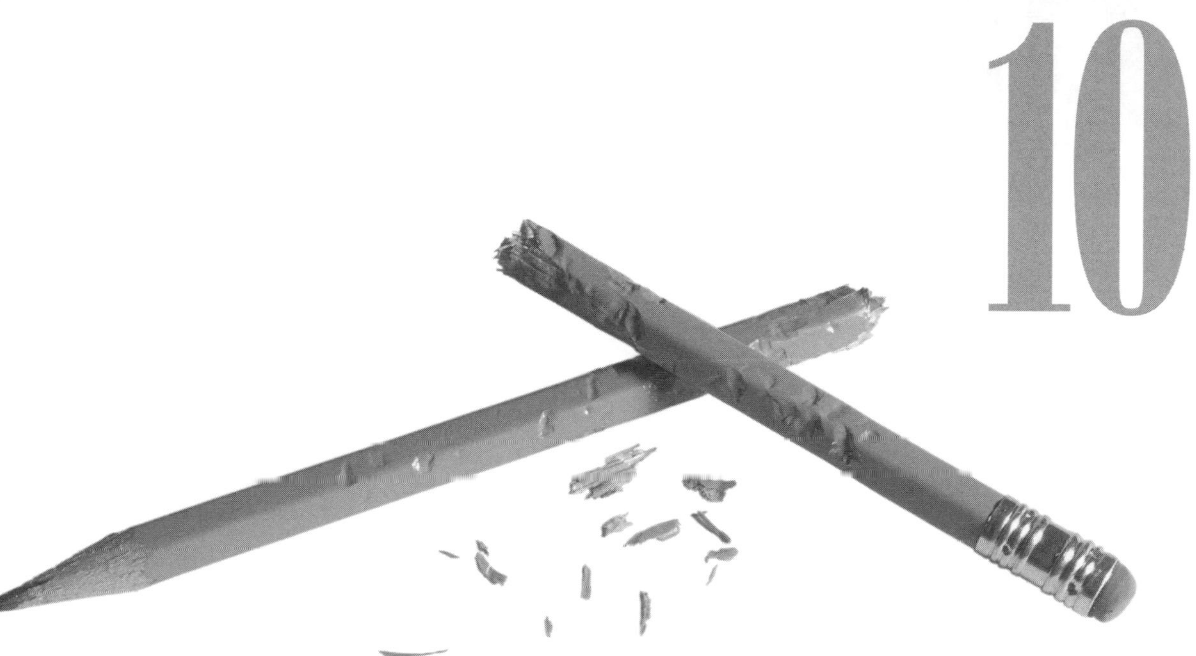

10 IF YOU WERE A TREE, WHAT KIND OF TREE WOULD YOU BE: COPING WITH DIFFICULT INTERVIEWS

Derek was starting to think he was going to have to take matters into his own hands. He'd been preparing for this interview for more than a week. And preparing for the job for a lot longer than that. He had dozens of great examples to share from the sales calls on which he'd accompanied the account executives and the presentations he'd made. He was confident that he had plenty of evidence to prove that he was right for an account executive spot.

So why wasn't Jill Zucker asking him about any of that? Why was she asking these questions that didn't seem to have anything to do with the job at all? The courses he'd taken in college, his opinion about the future of cellular communications. They'd talked for 20 minutes already, and Derek was sure that Jill hadn't learned anything about him that would show he would be successful as an account executive.

He knew that Jill was under a lot of pressure—some of the voice mail messages he'd gotten from her had been sent at midnight or six in the morning. He couldn't figure out why she seemed so uninterested in this interview. She

was the one who had scheduled it, after all. Her mind seemed to be elsewhere.

After each of his answers, a long silence would pass, as if Jill were struggling with what to ask next. And every time she spoke, Derek felt more confused and frustrated. He was trying to think of a way to give her the information he'd prepared—all of his sales and presentation experiences—without seeming rude by not answering her questions.

His thoughts were interrupted by her next inquiry: "What do you think are your weaknesses?"

"Hmm," he said out loud, "I would have to say that I tend to be something of a workaholic. And a perfectionist."

He stopped. Those were his weaknesses. There wasn't much more to say. Suddenly it occurred to him to add, "You know, recently I was working on a project where those elements of my working style came into play. My team almost missed a deadline because I was obsessed about adjusting a detail in one of our proposals."

"Really," Jill replied, leaning in toward him a bit. "Tell me more about what happened."

"There was a graphic that was supposed to represent the system architecture for a communications design. Even though we had signed off on the graphic, I thought it wasn't quite right. I took it back to the graphic artist and explained to her that each of the subsystems connected to the central database. The graphic needed to show that. Because we had said the graphic was final, she had archived the files and moved to another project."

"How did it turn out?" Jill asked.

"She couldn't just drop everything on her current project to make my change. It took a while for her to find time to retrieve the files, but she made the correction and we got the proposal out on time. In fact, we got the contract. But I learned something from the experience. I need to do a better job understanding other people's priorities and accommodating them. Just because I spend long hours at the office working out every detail of a project . . . well, not everyone works that way. And if I had to do it all over again, I'd approach the situation differently. I'd make my image of the graphic more clear up front, and I'd ask for the artist's help in figuring out the best way to represent the subsystems' relationships to the database, instead of making it seem as if she had made a mistake."

"Tell me about your strengths, then."

"I pride myself most on my ability to manage multiple projects. When I was leading the design team working on the X-46 project, I had two other designs going at the same time, with similar deadlines and scopes. I posted huge charts on my office door to track the status of each project. They helped me organize everything that was going on, and anyone requesting a status report could have one instantly. All three projects were completed on time."

"What is another strength?" asked Jill.

Derek was tempted to say, "Being interviewed." He had a strong urge to pat himself on the back. He'd used some of his prepared examples, even when Jill hadn't explicitly asked for them. He suddenly had the feeling that the interview was going well.

"Actually," Derek said, "I've found that my ability to learn is a real strength. When I decide to learn a new skill and have the opportunity to practice it hands on, it takes me very little time to catch on. For example, I didn't have much experience in making sales presentations, but when I decided I wanted to learn how to do it effectively, I jumped in with both feet.

"I started where I felt comfortable—with presentations to my team—and used their feedback to refine my style. I sought coaching from people I'd identified as talented speakers. I even rented a video camera so I could record myself and watch my performance. Since I started working on my skills, I've participated in more than a dozen sales presentations as a technical support person for some of the new account executives. All those presentations earned positive responses from the AEs and from clients. At least six have resulted in sales."

Jill smiled. Derek was certainly doing quite a sales job. ★

Vague or Unclear Questions

Some interviewers just love to ask vague questions:

- Tell me about yourself.
- Why should we hire you?
- What are your strengths and weaknesses?
- What have you done that you are really proud of?
- What do people say about you?

Vague questions are poor because they don't bring out specific behavioral data that could be related to the dimensions for a job. They require the interviewer to interpret the data—and that interpretation is more often wrong than right.

Don't worry about these questions. An interviewer usually comes up empty by asking such imprecise questions to run-of-the-mill applicants. But you are a prepared applicant. You have a list of key dimensions that you want to bring out. Now is your opportunity. Whenever you hear a vague question, ask yourself, "What are those five key dimensions I want to bring out?" and mention one of them. You can't go wrong.

Illegal or Discriminatory Questions

There is another category of truly wrong questions. These are questions that break the laws that protect people from discrimination based on gender, race, age, color, national origin, religion, disabilities, etc. The laws of the United States and many other countries clearly state that all questions in an interview must be directly job related. For example, an interviewer cannot ask questions about your family situation because your family doesn't have anything to do with how well you would do a job.

Note: A professional psychologist conducting a clinical interview of an applicant can get away with a question (such as one about your family) that is not directly job related. A psychologist is qualified to use such information to better understand underlying motivations that are job related.

The following are areas protected by federal and state laws in the United States:

- Age
- Children/Family status
- Disability/Medical history
- Marital status
- Race/National origin
- Religion
- Gender

Most interviewers who ask illegal questions don't intend to discriminate. However, they shouldn't ask such questions, and you do not have to answer them. What do you say if your interviewer asks an illegal question?

Your best response is to explore the meaning behind the question and speak to that, rather than to the illegal question. For example, if you were seeking a job that required extensive travel and the interviewer asked you about your marital status or the number of children you have under 16, he or she would probably be trying to find out if child care is an issue.

An appropriate answer would be, "I am sure you are concerned about my ability to travel. Let me assure you that I have made all necessary arrangements so that I can travel the amount of time that you indicated was common for this job. I have traveled even more than that in my last two jobs." Without confronting the issue of the illegal question, you have provided a valuable behavioral example and lessened the interviewer's anxiety.

Your best response is to explore the meaning behind the question and speak to that, rather than to the illegal question.

Often people will ask an illegal question inadvertently in making conversation. An interviewer might say, "Oh, DeCario. Is that an Italian name?" Here, if you wish, you could deflect the question with a comment such as, "I'm sure you've worked with people of all nationalities."

It is usually better not to confront an interviewer about an illegal question. Using your sense of humor or diverting the interviewer by indirectly answering the question will often defuse the situation.

Keep in mind, however, that your interviewer represents the organization. If you are being asked offensive or openly discriminatory questions, you might reconsider whether you'd like to work for the organization. You also might have legal recourse if you feel that discriminatory interview practices cost you a job for which you were well qualified.

What Not to Share

Interviewers should not ask non-job-related questions and similarly, you should not offer non-job-related information that might inadvertently bias an interviewer. For example, you probably shouldn't bring up the fact that you are responsible for 10 young children (five are yours and five are your spouse's). Because it is illegal for the interviewer to explore that information with further questions, the interviewer might be left with doubts about your ability to travel, willingness to work late, etc. Nor is it appropriate for you to disclose that you are going through a nasty divorce or some other personal crisis. What point would you be making? You would only be distracting the interviewer from the primary task: collecting data about dimensions important to job success.

On the other hand, if your personal situation will affect your job, it is appropriate to discuss these issues. It is best to discuss job-related issues up front, rather than let a problem affect your performance after you are hired.

Questions Designed to Measure Your Tolerance for Stress

Some interviewers use difficult questions to test how an individual reacts to stress; other interviewers use them because they are nasty people. Either way, stress-inducing questions are seldom an effective way for the interviewer to get information because the stress you feel in the interview is generally quite different from the kind of stress you would face on the job.

An interviewer might apply stress by ridiculing your answers or belittling your accomplishments:

"Oh, that is only a state university."

The interviewer might emphasize your faults:

"You mean you never thought that the programming might not be done on time, and you didn't have any alternative plans?"

Anyone would feel stress when facing such a question. Our best advice is for you to recognize what the interviewer is doing and resolve that you are not going to let such tactics get to you.

If several interviewers from the same organization use the same tactics, you might ask yourself what organizational value they are expressing and whether you would want to work in the organization.

Questions About Competitive or Confidential Information

If you are interviewing with a competitor of your present employer, you might be asked to reveal confidential information:

"Can you tell me about some of the products under development in your company?"

Although interviewers should not use the interview situation to gain competitive information, it still happens. Your best response is to say that you can't provide that information because it is competitive, and you want to respect your obligation to your employer.

Confidential information includes lists of clients, information about new products, and financial data. Don't disclose any information that isn't accessible to the public.

Take care not to reveal confidential information when you are giving your STAR examples. Your openness could be misinterpreted. Avoid referring to customers or products with proper names; instead, use general terms, such as "a major client" or "one of our software packages."

Negatives in Your Background

Another difficult interview experience involves confronting negatives in your background. Derek was concerned that the interviewer would focus on his lack of formal experience or training in sales and marketing. Tom worried that his lack of an advanced degree would cause the interviewer to form a poor opinion about him before he even began speaking. Sara feared that her lack of work experience would cause her interviewer to overlook her qualities.

Most people get nervous before a job interview. Those uneasy feelings can cause us to think negatively about ourselves and the outcome of the interview. Remember that there are few "perfect" candidates out there—they've already found "perfect" jobs and are no longer looking. The other candidates for the position you're seeking are feeling just as nervous as you are. They've identified their own flaws that they fear will keep them from getting the job.

The best way to overcome a potential negative in your background is to be up front about it and use STAR examples to demonstrate how your strengths in other areas, such as high motivation to work or ability to learn, overcome the weakness.

Lack of Related Experience

Examine your dimension profile for comparable skills. While Derek didn't have sales experience, he was used to selling his ideas. The skills he used to pitch his design ideas were the same skills he'd need to sell products to clients.

Lack of Work Experience in General

Draw STAR examples from other aspects of your life—school, family life, or volunteer work for your community or place of worship. Sara had limited work experience, but her work on the student newspaper in college gave her impressive STAR examples.

Lack of Education or Advanced Degree

Emphasize the skills you've developed through on-the-job training and other experiences. Give STAR examples of your ability to learn and apply new concepts and the job-related knowledge and skills you have developed.

Show how you have changed since you last attended school. Describe how your attitude and work ethic have developed and give a STAR example.

Poor Academic Performance or a Degree from a Lesser Known School

Even if academics weren't your "thing," you probably have other skills and interests that capture your imagination. Concentrate on the skills that will be useful for the job you want and be prepared with STAR examples of your strength in those areas. Confront the issue with a statement such as, "I often had a hard time learning things by rote. I tend to be a hands-on learner." And follow this up with a strong STAR example of your ability to learn. Be honest and direct, and then move on.

Frequent Job Changes

Acknowledge your history up front and discuss what you've learned from your diverse experiences. If possible, find a common thread in your experience. For example, you might summarize your background by saying, "In all of these positions, I had the opportunity to work closely with customers," and offer multiple STAR examples. Be clear about your intentions with the job you're pursuing. Is this the job you want to stick with? How or why is this job different? Motivational fit facets can be important here.

Gap in Employment History

Again, it's usually best to acknowledge your history up front. If you were looking for work during the gap in your work experience, say so and, if appropriate, give a STAR example about an important, job-related dimension. For example, mentioning the skills you employed in your search during this period might demonstrate that you are highly motivated, a hard worker, and good at planning and time management.

If you took time off to travel, tell about what you learned from the experience. A STAR on how you applied that learning in a work situation would be a real plus.

Got Fired/Quit Job

Share what you learned from the experience. For example, if you were laid off, perhaps you gained insight into yourself or decided to pursue more training. If you quit a job that wasn't right for you, describe how you researched a new field. In today's workplace, job changes are increasingly common. There's no need to feel ashamed about or to hide anything that happened to you as long as you can demonstrate that you've learned from the experience.

Dimensional-Based Negative Questions

Good interviewers sometimes ask specific questions that relate to shortcomings and negative behaviors such as, "Tell me about a time when details have fallen between the cracks (planning and organizing)," or "Tell me about a problem you had with another associate (interpersonal skills)."

DDI consultants train interviewers to seek such information from candidates. The purpose is to gather information about the candidate's flexibility and ability to learn from mistakes, and also to see how the person followed up or made improvements to eliminate future mistakes. Everyone makes mistakes. A candidate who claims to never have made a mistake instantly loses credibility.

Be prepared for the interviewer to ask you follow-up questions about negatives. If the interviewer has been trained by DDI, he or she will seek a STAR, then a second STAR, and then a third STAR. An effective interviewer will know if you're telling the truth by how believable each STAR is.

Intelligent Answers for Dumb Questions

During Jill's interview with Derek, she asked some questions that Derek found difficult to answer. We've all been asked "dumb" questions, from what our favorite color is to what kind of animal we'd like to be. Dumb questions don't always have to be met with dumb answers. Remember that your goal is to give your interviewer as much information (behavioral data) about yourself as you can. Your turnaround responses, then, should focus on providing a STAR example instead of theoretical information.

Theoretical or general questions don't give the interviewer real data about you; instead, the decision to hire or promote will be based on impressions and suppositions. Because the goal of the interview is to make a match—a win-win situation in which the organization gets the best candidate and you get the job you'll do best in—your answers should be providing proof for the match. This all comes back to (surprise, surprise) the practice of giving STAR examples. Here are some samples.

Interviewer: What three words best describe you?

"The words that come to mind are analytical, independent, and creative. I'm a very process-oriented thinker. I like to understand things thoroughly before I make decisions. But once I've analyzed the situation, I like to act on my own because I'm usually confident about the decision my analysis has led me to.

"And I do tend to generate my own solutions—I like to think creatively and do things in new ways. It keeps things interesting.

"When I volunteered in an advocacy program at family court, I was asked to help come up with a way to encourage mothers to pursue child support claims. Many women were put off by the forms and processes and were confused about what was required of them. I began by sitting in the waiting area and talking to the people who'd come in to file claims. I identified several points that held people back.

"One frequent comment was that a person needed an attorney to pursue support and that welfare benefits would be cut if child support was paid. I surveyed each person who came in about these ideas to get a feel for how common these misconceptions were. Then I made note sheets clarifying these points in several languages. We attached them to the top of the forms.

"Next, I put together a 'help line' of volunteers who could help applicants with forms and answer questions. I contacted the director of a

local public interest law firm who was willing to secure funding for such an effort. This year I saw my idea come to life, and I'm thrilled with the results. Applications are up by more than 10 percent."

Interviewer: What would you do if . . . ?

Give a STAR example of something you actually did in a similar situation.

"I faced a similar situation when . . ."

If none comes to mind, ask your interviewer to clarify the question for you.

"I'm not sure how to answer that question. I've never really been in a situation like that. What kinds of skills would you expect an employee to demonstrate if that happened?"

Ask for more information about the situation until you have enough to effectively answer the question. The interviewer will be impressed by your questions. Pick up on the skills the interviewer is looking for and draw your STAR example from them.

Interviewer: What do you think about . . . ?

Interviewers who ask this question are trying to get at motivational fit but are doing it poorly. If your interviewer asks, "How do you feel about customer service?" or "How do you feel about working in a fast-paced environment?" it's best to answer honestly. If you do not feel comfortable working at a fast pace, say so: "I prefer a more relaxed pace."

This bears repeating: Lying in an interview is never worthwhile. At worst, your interviewer will catch you. At best, you'll be hired for a job for which you are ill qualified or ill suited. Either way, you're worse off than if you told the truth. If you can truthfully answer positively, give your interviewer proof by giving STAR examples:

"I've always thought of myself as a customer-service-oriented person, but helping out in my brother's restaurant really taught me what customer service means. Sometimes, I was so tired that I just wished all the customers would go home, but I had to learn to get past that feeling.

"People come to a restaurant to relax and enjoy themselves—it's about service as much as about food. Sometimes that means adjusting the air conditioner so it doesn't blow down a customer's neck. Sometimes it means taking a dish back to the kitchen until it's perfect. Working for tips gives you instant feedback—you always know how you're doing.

"One night I waited on a large party—a group of friends out for a night on the town—and

even though I was tired, their spirit of fun was contagious. By letting go of the feeling of drudgery that I usually had about my job, I was able to give great service. Instead of thinking about what to do as a server, I thought about what I'd like if I were out for the evening. I anticipated their needs without hovering."

Interviewer: Tell me three good things and three bad things about yourself.

You might be tempted to fall back on a canned response or a vague statement. All of us can come up with at least three good things about ourselves. With some advance work, you should also be able to come up with STARs for those qualities. You might have trouble articulating the latter part of this request—the bad things. You might not think of anything to say or offer a positive cloaked as a negative such as, "I work too hard," or "I'm too much of a team player."

We all have bad points, shortcomings—things we'd like to change about ourselves. Claiming to be perfect will detract from your credibility. Be honest, but be sure to give examples of how you are overcoming the negatives. If you're a procrastinator, mention what you're doing to address this tendency, such as carrying an electronic organizer or keeping a detailed to-do list.

Interviewer: If you were a ______, what would you be?

You might be asked, "If you were an animal/tree/bird/flower/color, what would you be?" The interviewer most likely won't be able to accurately interpret your truthful response. Usually, such a question is asked by an inexperienced interviewer to fill time. The person probably doesn't really care about the answer.

One way to handle this question is to return to the aspects of your dimension profile that you want to emphasize:

"I'm not sure I know what kind of tree I would be, but I'd be one that showed a lot of initiative."

When answering this or any other dumb question, keep your tone friendly. If you encounter a number of similar questions, your interviewer is probably inexperienced and nervous. You can handle this situation by keeping yourself focused on the topics you decide are important.

Turnaround Phrases

How can you turn around an interview that has reached an impasse or inspires little communication? Derek was at a loss for something to say; he felt like he was failing a test. Jill also felt that the meeting was going nowhere, but her instinct was to fault Derek for his inability to keep up the conversation.

Don't give up on an interaction that isn't going as you'd hoped it would. Understand that just as you are under pressure to find a job, your interviewer is under pressure to find the right candidate. Acknowledging this pressure and making an effort to work through it is often the best way to let your interviewer know that you are serious about the position.

Another way to demonstrate your appreciation for the interviewer's time is to check on how you're doing. Midway through your interview (or during a natural pause), ask the interviewer if you are providing clear, appropriate information. If you're not, you have the opportunity to improve your performance on the spot. Be sure to apply any suggestions the interviewer might offer. Asking for feedback and then ignoring it is worse than not asking at all.

It's a daunting task to assert yourself in a lackluster interview. Most people want to exit an awkward situation as quickly as possible. We might "just say no" when asked if we have additional questions or comments, thinking that's the best method of damage control. On the contrary, asking questions can refocus an interview that's gone badly. The following are some sample turnaround phrases that can refocus an interview:

"I'd like to learn more about this position. My impression is that it would involve a lot of [use a dimension here]. What else can you tell me about it?"

Let your interviewer confirm your impression and then offer a STAR example of your strength in this dimension.

Or if your interviewer corrects your mistaken impression, pick up on the new information and continue the conversation by offering a relevant STAR or further exploring the job. You might say:

"I see. I understand that more clearly now. Thanks. I think the opportunity to use those skills would be highly appealing to me. In my last position [offer a STAR example here] . . ."

Here are examples of other turnaround phrases:

"I know we've been pressed for time here, but I would like to spend a moment or two telling you about what I think is one of my real strengths." [Offer a STAR example.]

"I work best when [offer information from your analysis of motivational fit] . . . It seems that there would be a lot of opportunities to work that way in this position. Is that right? [Offer STAR examples of behaviors that demonstrate your matching motivations.] What else can you tell me about the work environment here?"

"I'd like to tell you about a project that I worked on in my last position (or as a student or volunteer). I think it illustrates the way I work best." [Remember to use the STAR format!]

"One of the things I'm most proud of is my ability to [discuss an important dimension related to your job success and offer one or two STAR examples] . . . "

Interruptions and Distractions

DDI asked people across the country about difficult interviews they had endured. A large number described interviews that were farces because of distractions: phone calls interrupting the interview, people coming into or working in the room where the interview was taking place, the interviewer frequently leaving the interview. One person reported that her interviewer took 20 phone calls during a one-hour interview. While this form of insensitivity is rare, you should know how to deal with it.

First, think what you are learning from the experience—about the individual and the job. If the interviewer will be your boss, you are getting a glimpse of how much attention and coaching you can expect on the job. The nature of the distractions can give you some clues about the pace of the job, the issues facing the organization, and how much freedom people have to make independent decisions. Does the interviewer seem to be making every decision for the people in the unit?

And it's a bad sign if the interviewer is unaware of the insensitivity of these situations. These insights might lead you to decide that the job is not for you especially if it is in a small department or a small company. If so, get out while you have a chance.

Before you are too hasty, however, look beyond the individual to the job and the organization. What about the other people that you have met?

Will you be working directly with the interviewer on the job? Could this just be a very bad day for the interviewer? If this is your first interview with an organization and if you want to give it a second chance, you might try the following:

- Ask to reschedule the interview by saying:

  "You seem really busy. I certainly know what it's like to have to conduct an interview when you've got a lot of other things to do. Can I come back later or some other time?"

Such a suggestion usually works if the interviewer has been apologetic about the interruptions. The person might be quite embarrassed and would be relieved for a way out of the situation.

- Seek another interviewer by saying:

  "You've been most helpful. I know how busy you are. Is there anyone else I could talk to about the position?"

Unprepared Interviewers and Organizations

DDI's survey of difficult interviews also uncovered stories of situations in which the candidate showed up for the interview, and no one expected him. Although unusual, these kinds of situations do happen:

- The candidate flies into town, finds that there's no hotel reservation, and the contact people at the organization are on vacation.

- The candidate arrives for an interview, but is not expected. People in the organization might try to set up some interviews, but, of course, the interviewers are unprepared and are trying to conduct the interview in the midst of busy schedules—often with their minds on other things.

These are organizational foul-ups, and they tell you things about the hiring organization that you shouldn't overlook. Just as we believe that the past behavior of the candidate is a good indication of future job behavior, we believe it is also true of an organization.

However, to err is human, and all organizations make mistakes in their handling of applicants. Such mistakes are especially common in young, fast-growing organizations that have outpaced the skills of their human resources departments. Thus, it might be worth giving the organization a second try, even if it means missing an extra day at work or making a second plane trip.

If you think it is worth the effort, volunteer to reschedule and make the most of the time in between to get additional information about the job and the organization. Make one or more of these requests of the people in the human resources department (or whomever you are dealing with):

- Ask for a tour of the facility.
- Ask to meet people who might be your peers. People at your peer level might be more available for interviews, because they probably don't do it every day and might be more willing to help.
- Ask if anyone is available to talk to you about the organization—not for an interview, just to help you gather facts. It's amazing what level of people you might speak to using this tactic.

Often, because the people in the organization feel bad about what you've undergone, they try to treat you extra well the second time. If they don't work hard to make your next visit hassle free, it's probably not the organization for you.

NOTES

DON'T CALL US, WE'LL CALL YOU: ENDING THE INTERVIEW ON A POSITIVE NOTE

11

Do You Have Any Questions?

Establish Next Steps

Make a Summary Statement

11 DON'T CALL US, WE'LL CALL YOU: ENDING THE INTERVIEW ON A POSITIVE NOTE

As he snapped together the last pieces of his display, Tom imagined JoAnne watching him. He was sure that she was behind this. At age nine, Lisa had decided that her parents, especially her father, were "uncool." And yet, she had invited Tom to the school's career fair. Yes, he was sure JoAnne had talked Lisa into it. So there he was, doing his best to show grade-school kids about high-tech component assembly.

This was the second time this week that Tom had been inside a school. Until two days ago, it had been five years since his last night course, an aborted attempt to earn his degree. He was proud of himself for going back. Tom knew he needed to build his confidence. He'd always been one to learn from his mistakes.

And his interview for the project management job had definitely been a mistake. The interview had gone badly from the start, but looking back on it, Tom was sure he'd really blown it at the end. Mr. Anderson had said, "I'd like to spend the remaining 15 minutes answering the questions you have about the position, Tom." And Tom had said that he didn't have any.

Tom wasn't sure what had made him say it, but, at that moment, he had just wanted to get out of that office and back to the plant. It was weeks before he would even discuss the interview—or the job he wasn't offered—with anyone. But when he did, he realized that his lack of a degree wasn't all-important, but it was a vital missing link.

Not having a degree ate away at his confidence. He could see that if he were going to move up in the world, he had to build in himself the kind of confidence he saw in the executives at GenEquip. They always sounded like they knew what they were talking about. They seemed to stand a head taller than everyone else.

When Tom explained his feelings to JoAnne, she had said, "Maybe it's time to do something." He hated it when she was right.

Walking into his business and strategic planning course at Hamburg College was one of the tougher things Tom had ever done. It was supposed to be one of the more challenging courses they offered. And the room was filled with students who looked to be in their early twenties. He spotted only one other student who looked about his age, and it turned out that she was in the wrong room. But Tom had stuck it out. And he was going back tonight. He was determined to ace the class.

As the gymnasium began to fill with fourth and fifth graders, Tom thought about his own elementary school days. He'd been a decent student; hard-working, people called him.

"Hey, Lisa!" His daughter had just walked by without so much as a wave. She turned, smiled at him, and continued to walk with her friends. One student's parents ran a bakery, and all the kids were headed to their booth for free cookies. Tom wondered if he'd get any takers for his demonstration of component assembly.

"Don't feel bad," the guy next to him spoke up, "my kids don't even smile at me."

They laughed, and Tom stepped out from behind the display table to introduce himself.

Paul Berry was from Diversified Products. Tom passed those offices every day on the way to work. It turned out that he and Paul had been crossing paths for years—one of those "small world" things. Paul's son had played in the same soccer league as Tom's girls; his wife was a social worker who had an office at the hospital where JoAnne worked.

As Tom had figured, there wasn't much use in trying to compete with the bakery. Or the surgeon (who had a skull and a spongy plastic model of a brain). Tom and Paul had plenty of time to get to know each other. They'd been talking for half an hour when Tom asked, "So, what do you do for DP, anyway?"

Paul's answer was almost inaudible. "Oh, you know how things are. Little of this, little of that," he said. Tom laughed in agreement, figuring that, like him, Paul had a job that he was trying to get promoted out of. He told Paul about his recent experience with the project management job.

"So, I'm trying to look at it as a learning experience. I'm taking a management course over at Hamburg. And I'm trying to brush up on my interviewing skills in case something else comes along. I figured out that I really need to practice talking about the things I've done. You know, giving examples. I mean, I've relived that last interview a million times."

It was true. Since the interview, Tom had thought of a thousand things he might have asked or points he might have made. He could have even raised the issue of his lack of a degree. He could have impressed Mr. Anderson with how much he had learned about the history of the project management initiative at GenEquip. He could have said or done pretty much anything, but he didn't. Instead he had said, "I think we've covered everything," and had stood up to leave. He'd spent a lot of time wondering how he could have been so stupid.

"Sounds like you're on the right track," said Paul.

Tom felt his face turn a bit red; he'd probably been boring the guy half to death. He quickly changed the subject back to kids' soccer. It had been almost an hour, and Tom had given his demonstration twice, both times to a kid whose mother worked at the plant. Paul checked his watch and declared that he had to get back to work.

On his way out Paul shook Tom's hand and gave him a business card. "Why don't you give me a call sometime. Maybe Diversified has a job that would be right for you—I'll keep my ears open." Tom gave a polite thank-you to his new friend. He was sure that nothing would come of Paul's offer, but he was pleased with his first "networking" experience. Tom stuffed the card in his pocket without a second glance.

The children were filing out of the gym; it was 10 minutes before dismissal. He spotted Lisa's dark curls once again and signaled for her to come over. She smiled and did not ignore him.

"How about I give you a ride home, and we stop for a snack on the way?"

She didn't answer right away, which he knew meant, "Thanks, but no thanks."

"OK," he tried again. "How about I give you some money for a snack, and you walk home with your friends?"

Lisa's face lit up as he reached into his pocket for a couple of dollars. As he handed her the cash, Tom noticed Paul's card. "Chief operating officer," he read aloud. He really was networking. ★

Do You Have Any Questions?

Interviews traditionally end with the interviewer asking, "Do you have any questions?"

Most interviewers want a candidate to ask meaningful questions when given an opportunity. They absolutely hate to hear, "I don't think so. I think we covered everything."

If you don't ask questions, it seems as though you never fully engaged in the interview. The interviewer knows that the time allotted makes it impossible to discuss every aspect of your qualifications and the job's requirements. Asking questions is your chance to collect important information about the job. Also, it's your opportunity to come back to the key dimensions that you planned to discuss and to make sure you provided the necessary STARs.

You might ask questions about two areas often not covered by interviewers and which might be important in helping you gather complete information on the job. The first area is the reporting structure of the job. Simply put, to

whom will you report and who will report to you? It's best to ask this question diplomatically:

"I'm not sure I have a full understanding of where this position fits into the organization. How is it connected to others in the department?"

A second area to pursue concerns issues that are important to determining your motivational fit for the position. Remember that motivational fit includes the task content of the job, the culture of the organization, and the physical location of your workplace. Gathering as much information as possible about these topics will be useful to you in deciding whether this is the right job for you. Also, your interest will indicate to your interviewer that you are serious about finding a position in which you can excel.

Most interviewers will be impressed that you've taken the time to analyze the job. Even if you're not right for this position, your interviewer might be more likely to consider you for another position within the organization.

If these areas have been covered to your satisfaction, there might be other questions for you to ask. For example, if you had identified a dimension as being important for the job and it was not covered, you could raise that subject:

"You said that there will be four or five people reporting to this position, but we didn't get a chance to talk about leadership. I am assuming that it would be important."

If your interviewer agrees, you've created an opening to give your STAR examples of your leadership abilities.

You also might find yourself in a situation in which you have given only one STAR for an important dimension, and you want to provide back-up data:

"I wanted to check if I gave you enough information on my ability to plan and my skills in project management. We touched briefly on those areas, but I've had a number of other experiences that I would be glad to share with you."

Also, you might realize that you handled a question poorly during the interview and you need to clarify the issue by providing another STAR example:

"When we talked about creativity, I mentioned only one example and that was when I was working on my own. As you know, I have been a team leader for five years, and my team has shown a lot of creativity that we all are proud of. Would that interest you?"

A good interviewer will pick up on that opportunity and ask you to give additional information.

If you've given all the STARs you've prepared and you feel that your interviewer has truly covered everything, you can use your question to summarize your key dimensions and double-check that you've covered the dimensions that are important to the interviewer:

"I tried to give you some information on my experience, my ability to learn languages, and my ability to run a multicultural organization. What other information would be helpful?"

Topics Not to Touch

Questions regarding salary, benefits, and vacations are best asked of people from the human resources department, not of the managers who will be making the final hiring decision. Don't use the limited time at the end of an interview for a discussion of these issues. It's often necessary to wait until you get a job offer to receive all details about the salary and bonus structure. If you have general questions, address them to the human resources associate with whom you originally spoke about the position.

Establish Next Steps

It's usually a good idea to ask if your interviewer requires any additional materials from you, such as transcripts, references, or work samples. As you close your interview, make final arrangements on where, when, and to whom you should send these materials.

The organization's human resources department should have already explained to you what happens next in the hiring process—another interview, some testing, a simulation—and when a decision is to be made. If you don't know this information, ask the appropriate person. By having a clear picture of the selection process, you'll be prepared for the next step—and you won't be worried if you don't hear from the organization until after the day they make the hiring decision.

Also, if you don't know, ask your interviewer when (and with whom) it would be appropriate for you to follow up about the status of the hiring decision.

Make a Summary Statement

If you can do it, close your interview by summarizing your strengths and how they fit with the organization's needs. You can prepare this statement in advance by using your three best-matched dimensions. Be sure that they are still the most relevant dimensions, because you might have received some additional information about the job during the interview. Your summary statement should be clear and simple:

"This position sounds like a great opportunity for me to continue to use and develop my project management skills. I'm very excited about it."

If you can do it, close your interview by summarizing your strengths and how they fit with the organization's needs.

Sometimes, interviews end abruptly: A critical phone call or meeting interrupts your interviewer, who offers an apology (maybe) and a quick handshake. You might not have the opportunity to use your summary statement. It's best to respect your interviewer's time by saying thank you and offering a graceful good-bye. You can include your summary statement in your follow-up note.

Keeping Your Coach Informed

If you have an inside coach, you should keep him or her informed of your progress. The coach will appreciate a call to report how your interview went. It also is a great opportunity to get some more coaching. This will keep the person on your side as an internal coach.

Saying Thank You

As you leave your interview, thank your interviewer as well as others you've been in contact with, such as an assistant or a receptionist. Thank them all for their time. Remember, these people could be your colleagues soon, and it's important for you to make a good impression.

You should send a thank-you letter to your interviewer as quickly as possible. If the hiring decision is a month or more away, it might be wise for you to follow up twice—once immediately after the interview and once just before the decision is to be made.

In short, thank everyone. And thank goodness it's over.

20/20 HINDSIGHT: LEARNING FROM THE INTERVIEW

12

Be Your Own Coach

Evaluate Your STAR Examples

Evaluate Your Preparation and Performance

12

20/20 HINDSIGHT: LEARNING FROM THE INTERVIEW

Jim Bodnar stood up from his chair and stretched with an enormous yawn. "Eleven-thirty and I'm going to bed," he declared. "Now this is the life."

Lately, Amanda too had come to think of a night's sleep as a luxury. She was already dozing on the couch. Curled into a ball, wrapped in a cotton blanket, she nearly disappeared when she slept. It was one of the things Jim loved about her. It was a relief to see her like this—so completely relaxed. Jim had seen his wife go through "phases" before—like when she had insisted on building the patio furniture herself. When Amanda decided on something, she'd argue her point until it wasn't worth discussing any further. But this job situation was different. She just wouldn't talk about it at all, and it worried him.

Amanda stood up lazily, ready to fall into bed. "We're such party animals," she yawned in response to his declaration.

Jim laughed and nodded. Things hadn't been this comfortable between them in quite a

while. He wasn't sure what had been bothering her, but he assumed it had to do with her new job. It couldn't have been his fault that she was barely speaking to him. He had things going on at work too. And he had offered to help out more at home.

On tiptoes Amanda kissed Jim on the cheek. It was a gesture understood between them to mean, "All is forgiven; let's move on."

The television off, the only light in the living room came from the glow of the streetlights outside. They looked at each other and saw only the outlines of the other's face, as if the wear of their years together had been erased. It was, as they would later joke, a "moment."

"Sometimes, I wonder what goes on in that head of yours," Jim said.

"You'll never know," she teased. She knew that her problems weren't solved. But she was going to do things right this time. For the first time since she'd started working for Willowbee's, she felt as if she were in control. She had decided to go after a job in the marketing department.

This time she'd do better at checking out the job; she'd ask questions; she'd make a list of job requirements and use it to be sure that she wanted the job and to help "sell" herself. Most of all, she'd learn something about the job interview process. She'd been lucky the last time, and she truly didn't know what she'd done right or wrong. But this time she was going to figure it out. And if the job in marketing didn't pan out, she knew there'd be other opportunities.

Be Your Own Coach

There is a saying that if you don't know where you are going, you will never know when you get there. That is certainly true about interviewing. If you don't have goals for what you want to communicate, you will never know how well you've done. To help you know where you're going, we've emphasized preparation as the key to successful interviewing. And to help you improve your preparation skills, we're including an evaluation exercise in which you can record how well you did in an interview and decide what areas you should concentrate on as you prepare for your next interview.

Any job interview is a learning experience. In an interview you have the opportunity to learn not only about a new job, but about yourself and about your own interviewing and communication skills. As soon as possible after an interview, take a few minutes to evaluate your performance. And remember, it's as important to learn from unsuccessful interviews as from successful ones.

Your self-critique after the interview is likely to be the only feedback you'll receive on your performance. Most interviewers will not give you a critique before they have made final decisions about candidates. Even an interviewer who calls to let you know that you didn't get the job usually will speak generally and be leery of providing information that might be misconstrued and turned into an EEOC charge.

Miss Something?

As you evaluate your performance, think about whether you discussed all your strengths (your best-matched dimensions) and whether you used most of the STAR examples you prepared.

Most important, you should be concerned about questions on dimensions for which you were not prepared. These dimensions might be idiosyncratic to the company, or they might be things that have suddenly become important in the field. For example, for years pharmaceutical salespeople did almost 100 percent of their business in one-to-one sales calls with physicians in their offices. Then, as physicians became aligned in delivery groups and other health care configurations, the sales opportunities to physicians turned into group meetings, facilitated by the salesperson, often with a noted outside expert as the main speaker. The requirements of the job changed radically, which probably surprised many job seekers.

It's Not Too Late

You're walking out the door and it hits you. Not the door, but the perfect answer for that question. You remember a time when you demonstrated just the skill the interviewer wanted to hear about. However, it's probably not a good idea to run back inside.

If you've failed to make a particular point or to discuss an important part of your dimension profile, you do have another chance. You can include the information in a prompt thank-you letter, or you could telephone the interviewer. Thank the person for the interview, say that you enjoyed meeting, and add that you weren't sure if you mentioned . . .

Also, if you have an interview coming up with another person from the organization, you can mention what you forgot before:

"You know, I'm not sure whether I discussed this with Ms. Smith, but I worked on a project . . ."

Your interviewers will talk to one another as they compile the data they've collected about you. They will share STARs on each dimension and share data on the STARs that they mutually obtained.

The advantage of doing your self-critique immediately after an interview is that you still have time to correct your mistakes.

The advantage of doing your self-critique immediately after an interview is that you still have time to correct your mistakes.

Listening Is All-Important
No matter how well prepared you were, your evaluation of the interview might show that the interviewer had a different set of dimensions than you had anticipated. You might have thought that because the company had undergone several downsizings, people would be cost conscious, and you prepared behavioral examples to illustrate dimensions that related to your skills in cost containment. Then during the interview, the interviewer might have stated that after its recent downsizing, the company was at an all-time-high profit level and was interested in growth opportunities.

Don't feel bad if something like this occurs. There's no way of anticipating these kinds of situations. This is why it is so important to listen and respond accordingly. No one can perfectly anticipate the dimensions for a job. Hitting 80 percent of them will put you ahead of your competitors for the job. In addition, your experience with STARs will make you better prepared to provide STARs for those dimensions you hadn't anticipated.

Let's look at how to evaluate an interview.

Evaluate Your STAR Examples

This exercise is designed to help you evaluate the effectiveness of the STAR examples you provided in your interview for the dimensions sought. In the left column list the dimensions sought by the interviewer. Don't list the dimensions you thought would be covered. List only the dimensions the interviewer was targeting with specific questions. You will probably have to do some guessing because it won't always be clear which dimension some questions cover.

In the middle column, jot down each STAR you provided for each dimension and, in the right column, rate each on whether it was recent, was job related, and demonstrated mastery or improvement. A "5" is a solid hit—a good STAR fulfilling all three criteria. A "1" would be a total miss.

As you fill in the worksheets, remember that this exercise is for your development only. Feel free to label dimensions with your own terms and use key words to remind you which STARs you used.

After you've completed your ratings, decide how well you did in the interview. Did you provide three STARs for the most important dimensions? Did you present your "shining" STARs? What was the quality of your STARs? How could you have improved the quality of your STARs? What did you forget to say? Can you think of any more STARs now?

Why take the time to do this follow-up exercise? The insights you gain will help you do a better job in your next interview. You might also discover that you need to pass on additional information to your interviewer through a phone call or thank-you letter.

If you don't have time to complete this exercise, at least ask yourself the questions on page 169, as a way of thinking about what you might do differently next time.

Evaluation Exercise

Evaluate Your STAR Examples

Dimension	Quality of STAR: Recent , Job Related, Demonstrates Mastery/Improvement	Rating 1=Low 5=High
	★ STAR 1	
	★ STAR 2	
	★ STAR 3	
	★ STAR 1	
	★ STAR 2	
	★ STAR 3	
	★ STAR 1	
	★ STAR 2	
	★ STAR 3	
	★ STAR 1	
	★ STAR 2	
	★ STAR 3	
	★ STAR 1	
	★ STAR 2	
	★ STAR 3	

Evaluate Your STAR Examples		
Dimension	**Quality of STAR:** **Recent , Job Related, Demonstrates Mastery/Improvement**	**Rating** **1=Low** **5=High**
	★ **STAR 1**	
	★ **STAR 2**	
	★ **STAR 3**	
	★ **STAR 1**	
	★ **STAR 2**	
	★ **STAR 3**	
	★ **STAR 1**	
	★ **STAR 2**	
	★ **STAR 3**	
	★ **STAR 1**	
	★ **STAR 2**	
	★ **STAR 3**	
	★ **STAR 1**	
	★ **STAR 2**	
	★ **STAR 3**	

Evaluate Your Preparation and Performance

Here are some questions to ask yourself as you evaluate how you did in one interview and prepare for another.

Your Preparation

1. Did you anticipate the knowledge/skill dimensions that would be evaluated?
2. Did you anticipate the behavioral dimensions that would be evaluated?
3. Did you anticipate the motivational dimensions that would be evaluated?
4. Did you find out as much information as you could about the company, the job, and the people who have held the job?
5. Overall, how successful was your preparation? From what sources did you gather information? Are there other sources of information that you might have used or that you should consider using in the future?

Your Performance

1. How would you evaluate your effectiveness in the interview?
2. What kind of rapport did you establish with the interviewer?
3. Did the interview seem to be rushed?
4. Did you cover your best-matched dimensions?
5. Did you use most of your shining STARs?
6. What dimensions did you prepare that you were unable to bring out?
7. What dimensions did the interviewer pursue for which you were not prepared?
8. How at ease were you in the interview?
9. Did you use the interviewer's name?
10. How prepared was the interviewer? What was the interviewer's impact on how you handled the interview?
11. What materials should you have brought along to substantiate a dimension?
12. What would you do differently next time?

NOTES

ELEVEN MONTHS LATER: A TUESDAY

13

13 ELEVEN MONTHS LATER: A TUESDAY

6:17 a.m.

Ed had customers who came by the Hav-a-Java Cafe every day on the way from the train station to Thompson Towers and the other office buildings on Second Avenue. Most of his customers were in a hurry. You could see them every day for a year, and they still wouldn't smile at you. It wasn't that they were hostile; it was just that they never noticed. One day you could be on a roll and have their orders ready before they even finished giving them, and the next day you could be a little hungover or something and be really slow, and there was no difference–just the same "thanks" or the same tight smile. It was enough to make Ed really hate the service industry. Besides, what he really wanted to do was direct films.

He made a point, though, of trying to get to know the ones who were just starting out–the ones who often paid for their breakfasts in change and, toward the end of a month, would order just coffee. Even though they almost never left anything in his "TIPS" basket, he had a soft spot for them. He always asked how they were doing, and he really wanted to know. A lot of them talked to him too. He liked to see them move up, to start wearing suits every day, to start coming in early in the mornings. It gave him a sense of progress, of time passing and things changing for the better. It was reassuring. It wasn't that he wanted that for himself, but he wanted to know that it still happened, that a person could still make it, that people still were getting lucky breaks. He felt sure his turn was coming.

Ed could always spot the person who had come into the city for a job interview.

Ed could always spot the person who had come into the city for a job interview—sporting a perfectly pressed suit and impeccably combed hair, checking a watch, ordering food but not eating it. It was easy to tell. He felt for those people. He knew it was hard. He couldn't see ever putting himself through all that agony, putting himself on the line like that. He got enough rejection from girls and producers.

Ed had just walked in, and he was setting up the counter. Jar of biscotti, basket of muffins. Stirrers, spoons, napkins. He hadn't gotten much sleep the night before, and he was counting the hours until he could go home and take a nap. He lost himself in the ritual of refilling the sugar and sweetener containers.

6:20 a.m.

Heart pounding, Derek Robertson tried the double doors. Locked. He checked his watch without noticing the time. He caught a glimpse of his panicked expression in the polished brass of the T-shaped door handle. Perturbed, he checked his watch again. It was exactly 20 minutes after, and he was standing in front of the Second Avenue entrance to the Thompson Towers complex. Just what they had agreed to. Twenty minutes after six. Six? A third time with the watch. It wasn't even 6:30 in the morning. He was an hour early.

"Sh . . . sugar," he muttered. It was an expression he'd picked up from Elaine and the kids. Even if he was standing in front of a locked door, he wasn't going to curse on a sales call.

"At least I'm not late," he thought miserably and headed back toward the train station to

grab a cup of coffee. He wasn't going to let his nerves get the best of him. Besides, those coffee places at the station were always open, and maybe he could find someone to talk to. He definitely needed to loosen up.

Ed rubbed his eyes. He had just finished the morning checklist. Six pots of coffee were brewing. The bagels had just been delivered. In walked his first customer.

"Hey, how are ya?" Ed asked, recognizing Derek as something of a regular.

"Oh, pretty good. Uh, I'll take a large coffee. You know, I haven't been here in a while. Looks like some new stuff." Derek pointed to the glass case that had replaced a section of the espresso bar.

"Yeah. We're branching out into more baked goods." He almost laughed as he thought how he had asked the manager just who the hell was going to buy an entire German chocolate cake. Besides, everyone was into low fat.

Derek took a seat and looked over his presentation notes. He wasn't enjoying the coffee—it was a little too strong—and was lost in his own thoughts when something startled him. Ed was sitting across the table from him.

"So, how've you been?" Ed asked, as if they were old buddies.

"Oh, uh, OK, I guess. You?"

"Well, you know, same old . . . but I'm thinking about going back to film school. I quit a while ago . . ."

"Well, I just changed jobs myself," said Derek. "I used to be an engineer, and now I'm in sales. It's been tough adjusting, but I'm having a good time with it. If you've got a goal, you should pursue it."

"Think so?" asked Ed.

"Definitely."

Ed nodded in agreement. Definitely.

7:58 a.m.

Derek straightened his tie. The LCD panel was in place on the overhead projector. The software was loaded, as was the video presentation. Landing this account would be a real coup. He imagined how it would feel to win this one—picturing victory had become a part of his ritual before a major presentation. It was one of the "tricks of the trade" his sales manager had taught him. Gene had been a salesman for years before becoming a manager and had been a terrific coach for Derek.

It wasn't that Derek thought he couldn't fail. But now that he had made it through some tough interviews, been through training, helped out on sales presentations—he was on his own with his own client.

Derek checked his watch just as his client, Dave Nye, asked, "All set?"

"Yeah, I think so."

"Terrific. I'll get the management team together and bring them in. I'm really excited about this idea, Derek. I think they'll go for it."

"Hope so. We've both put a lot of time into designing a communication system that will work for all of your field associates."

Dave nodded. He knew he never would have gotten his idea off the ground without Derek's implementation plan. The management team seemed enthusiastic, even though the price tag was substantial.

One by one the team members entered the conference room; each shook hands with Derek and took a seat, as if seats had been assigned.

"Are we ready to get started?" Derek asked.

Dave nodded and Derek took the sign. "I want to thank you all for taking the time to join me today. I'd like to introduce you to Milletech's new product."

8:24 a.m.

Sara's steps were quick but uneven. In her dress shoes she had trouble keeping up with the pace of her fellow commuters, and she nearly lost her balance as she pulled open the door to the coffee shop. She was preparing herself for her morning meeting. Though a senior account executive was managing the MacDougal's account, Sara had contributed to the presentation from start to finish—researching competitors, doing market studies, even generating ideas for promotional campaigns. She felt like she was coming into her own. Finally.

Her progress had certainly taken longer than she had planned. A year ago, she'd interviewed for a junior assistant account executive position and been turned down. After three interviews and a ton of tests, ZIPR had offered her a job as an administrative assistant. Though she'd spent almost two years swearing that she'd never do clerical work, Sara's AA job had been both a challenge and a learning experience. And after about six months, she'd gained the experience she lacked with clients and in project work. When a JAAE spot opened up, she breezed through her interviews.

"Large iced hazelnut—half decaf—with skim milk." Sara wondered how long she would have to come here before she could say with confidence, "The usual." It was one of those things she'd always wanted to say like, "Follow that cab." She decided to test the waters by seeing if the guy behind the counter recognized her.

"So," she began, as he turned to pour the coffee, "how are you today?" Her question trailed off as she realized she did not know his name.

Stirring her drink with a straw before handing it across the counter, Ed decided to lie. It was the polite thing to do. "Oh, pretty good. You?"

She nodded. "Great. Hey, by the way, I come in here every morning, and I never got your name. I'm Sara."

"Sara, I'm Ed. Nice to meet you."

Absurdly, they shook hands. And laughed at themselves. Behind Sara, a line was forming. She noted this with embarrassment, paid for her coffee, and left quickly.

"See ya," she said and she would—until the day she could send her administrative assistant out for coffee. But, she decided, she would never do that. Besides, Ed was sort of handsome in an underemployed sort of way. Since the

desperate part of her job search was over, she could make him her next project. He'd certainly get along with Dan.

5:40 p.m.

It had been his first day on the new job, and though he had loved it, Tom was eager to head home. He was sure that JoAnne had planned a celebration. He thought he might pick up a bottle of wine. He headed out the revolving door with what might be called a "spring" in his step.

Checking his watch, Tom realized he wouldn't have time to search out a liquor store and still catch the express train. With a slight nod of disappointment, he headed for the station. JoAnne would probably think of everything, anyway. She usually did.

Except dessert. He hated that low-fat stuff. And he didn't care how she dressed it up—fruit was not dessert.

A few steps shy of the station, he thought of the perfect thing. He'd spotted a German chocolate cake in the glass case when he'd stopped for coffee. He was sure it would still be there.

"Hey," he said, "how much for the cake?"

"Three dollars a slice," Ed said definitively, though he had no earthly idea what the price was supposed to be.

"No, I mean for the whole thing," Tom said.

"Oh, right, sorry. Uhhh . . . thirty bucks."

"Great, I'll take it."

Ed had just made the biggest sale of his long day. And the easiest. A lot of people couldn't even decide what flavor coffee they wanted, and this guy just marched in and bought a cake. Ed liked that.

☆ ☆ ☆ ☆ ☆ ☆

JoAnne rubbed her neck and opened her eyes. Tom would be home soon, and she had wanted to do something nice for him—have dinner on the table and maybe a bottle of wine. But she'd fallen asleep—just resting her eyes for a moment, she thought—and then woke up an hour later. She got up from the couch, stretched, and grabbed the pile of menus from the top of the fridge. At least there was time to order in.

6:11 p.m.
"Hey, beautiful," Tom said as he walked in. It was what he always said.

JoAnne was opening the last of the foil and plastic containers that had come from Umberto's. "Hey, yourself," she said. "How was the first day on the job?"

"You know," Tom said, loosening his tie, "it was pretty good. And," he said revealing the white box he'd been hiding behind his back, "I baked you a cake."

A year ago he'd almost given up hope of being promoted, but he'd done it. This time he'd really done it. The "A" he'd made in the management course he took at the college had given him confidence he'd never had. So much of what he'd done all his life was about managing people, planning, and making decisions—he just hadn't quite realized it.

"I've got to give Joe a call. He's the one who got me started on this whole thing, and I'm really going to miss working with him. But this team I'm heading at Diversified seems like a great bunch of people too. I think it was the right move, Jo, I really do."

JoAnne smiled at him. It was a look that combined joy, relief, and pride.

"C'mon," she laughed, "I've been slaving over a hot stove all day. Let's have dinner. Then you can call Joe."

6:32 p.m.
Amanda had made four lists. The first covered everything that Jim and the kids would need to know while she was away, from emergency phone numbers and her travel itinerary to the recipe for her favorite dessert (just in case they wanted to surprise her when she got home). List number two covered everything her colleagues would need to know in her absence—the details of the projects she was working on and the locations of her files, along with contact information in case of anything "really major."

List number three—the one she was clutching—detailed everything she had packed and her outfits for the trip. Amanda was certain she had everything; it was the third time she'd checked, but she just wanted to be sure. Three bathing suits with sarongs and sandals. Five evening outfits with open-toed shoes (she'd gotten a pedicure). A shawl and a silk blazer in case of cool breezes. An extra bag folded into the pocket of her suitcase, just in case they did a lot of shopping. With a nod of satisfaction, she snapped the list back into place in her organizer's three-ring binder.

And list number four—where was it?—included all the things she must do on vacation.

Her life was virtually unrecognizable from what it had been.

It was the first vacation Amanda had had since starting to work again, and it had to be perfect. She had paid for it, after all.

The elusive final list turned up underneath her desk blotter. She reviewed it with a smile. Jim wanted a box of hand-rolled cigars and had included an address in Tampa where they could be found. Her mother wanted a souvenir spoon for her collection, while Jim's father wanted an official cap from the local baseball team. The kids had listed their requests for mementos, and at the bottom of the list, Amanda had added a final reminder to herself: Take a breath!

She was almost ready to head for the airport. She'd have just enough time to stop for a cup of coffee at the cafe down the block and hail a cab. As usual, Amanda had timed the day perfectly. She was sure that she would arrive at the airport with at least 30 minutes to spare.

Amanda strode confidently into the coffee house. "A large coffee—black. And, actually, I'll take a decaf. I'm going on vacation."

Ed let out a sharp laugh. He drank decaf at work, but vacation—that he wanted to stay awake for.

The woman was carrying a briefcase and pulling one of those suitcase-on-wheels things behind her. Ed figured it would take her a while to find her wallet, but she effortlessly produced exact change from the pocket of her blazer.

Maybe it was the boy scout "dropout" in him, but he really admired preparedness. This woman impressed him.

6:45 p.m.

As the taxi driver inched toward the tollbooth, Amanda thought about the slow but steady progress she'd made in her career over the past months. Her life was virtually unrecognizable from what it had been. And now, in celebration of her new position, a Florida vacation with her best friend Judith. As the driver approached the exit ramp for the airport, Amanda checked her organizer one last time. Did she have her business cards? Judy would definitely want a card from Willowbee's new associate director of marketing.

7:01 p.m.

Ed locked the door behind him and headed home. This double-shift thing had to stop. They really needed to hire someone else. But who would want the stupid job? It's black coffee this and iced coffee that. The highlight of his day was when someone ordered a mocha. That took three whole minutes to make.

Come to think of it, why did he want this stupid job? It was at that moment, on the corner of Second and Broad, that Ed decided to look for another job. A real job.

One of his customers had told him about a book he could read about how to find the right job, but he figured he'd just wait for the movie. ✯

APPENDIXES

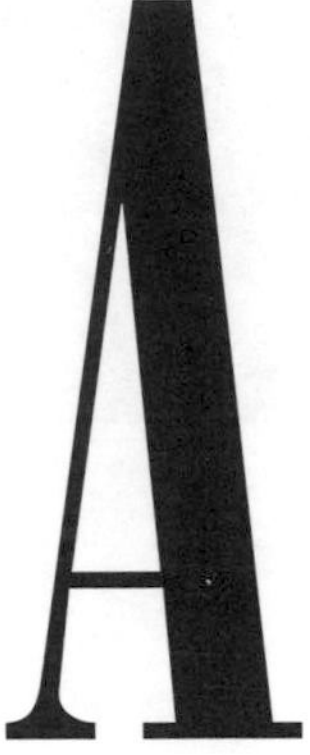

TOP BEHAVIORAL DIMENSIONS FOR ALL JOBS (WHAT INTERVIEWERS ARE LOOKING FOR)

The following list will aid your thinking about the behavioral dimensions related to success in the jobs in which you are interested. Although this list should provide 80 to 90 percent of the behavioral dimensions you need in your planning, you still need to determine the additional behavioral dimensions that are unique to the job or the organization. For example, formal presentation, personal impact, negotiation, risk taking, strategic thinking, or visionary leadership might be critical to the position you are seeking.

You also need to determine the knowledge/skill and motivational fit dimensions. They are much more specific to the job or organization. Use your knowledge of the organization, information provided by internal coaches, library research, and your interviewing skills to determine those dimensions.

Personal Dimensions

Adaptability—Maintaining effectiveness when priorities change, when new tasks are encountered, and when dealing with individuals who have different views and approaches; effectively performing in different environments, cultures, and locations, and when working with different technologies and levels of individuals.

Building Trust—Instilling confidence and credibility through actions and communications.

Continuous Learning and Growth—Assimilating and applying in a timely manner new job-related information that may vary in complexity; possessing intellectual agility needed to learn new concepts and tasks; showing eagerness and enthusiasm for learning new tasks and taking on additional responsibilities; taking the initiative in development activities; seeking and accepting feedback and coaching.

Creativity/Innovation—Generating creative solutions that were implemented and made an organizational difference; questioning traditional approaches to work; accepting and encouraging the innovation of others.

Energy—Consistently maintaining a high activity or productivity level; sustaining long work hours.

Initiative—Asserting one's influence over events to achieve goals; self-starting rather than accepting passively; taking action to achieve goals beyond what is required; being proactive.

Integrity—Maintaining and promoting social, ethical, and organizational norms; complying with company standards and ethical principles.

Stress Tolerance—Maintaining stable performance under pressure or opposition (such as time pressure or job ambiguity); relieving stress in a manner that is acceptable to the person, others, and the organization.

Tenacity—Staying with a position or plan of action until the desired objective is obtained or no longer reasonably attainable.

Interpersonal Dimensions

Coaching—Facilitating the development of others' knowledge and skills; providing timely feedback to help them reach goals.

Communication—Expressing thoughts, feelings, and ideas effectively in individual and group situations (including nonverbal communication); presenting ideas effectively when given time for preparation (including use of visual aids); clearly expressing ideas in memoranda, letters, or reports that have appropriate organization and structure and correct grammar, language, and terminology; adjusting language to the characteristics and needs of the audience.

Teamwork/Building Partnerships/Collaboration—Working collaboratively and cooperatively with others; building relationships; working effectively with team or work group or those outside the formal line of authority (e.g., associates, senior managers) to accomplish organizational goals; taking actions that respect the needs and contributions of others; contributing to and accepting the consensus; subordinating own objectives to the objectives of the organization or team.

Valuing Diversity—Appreciating and leveraging the capabilities, insights, ideas, and efforts of all individuals; working effectively with individuals of diverse style, ability, motivation, or viewpoint.

Leadership Dimensions (You don't have to be a formal leader to use these dimensions. Many progressive organizations want all employees to be leaders.)

Leadership and Influence—Using appropriate interpersonal styles and methods to inspire and guide individuals (direct reports, peers, team members, and senior managers) toward goal achievement; modifying behavior to accommodate tasks, situations, and individuals involved.

Meeting Participation/Leadership—Using appropriate meeting participation and facilitation styles and methods to guide participants toward a meeting's objectives; modifying behavior according to tasks and individuals present.

Sharing Responsibility—Allocating decision-making authority and task responsibilities to appropriate subordinates; utilizing subordinates' time, skills, and potential effectively; creating a sense of ownership of job or projects by providing clear expectations, control of resources, responsibility, and coaching; offering help without removing responsibility.

Decision-Making Dimensions

Decision Making—Identifying and understanding issues and problems; utilizing effective approaches for choosing a course of action or developing appropriate solutions; taking action that is consistent with available facts, constraints, and probable consequences.

Decisiveness—Making timely decisions, rendering judgments, taking action when appropriate, and committing to a side or position.

Planning and Organizing—Establishing a course of action for self and others to accomplish a specific goal; planning proper assignments of personnel and appropriate allocation of resources.

Business/Sales Dimensions

Customer Orientation—Effectively meeting customer needs; building productive customer relationships; taking responsibility for customer satisfaction.

Global Perspective—Appreciating the opportunities and problems inherent in implementing organizational initiatives in countries/cultures around the world; taking into consideration marketing, manufacturing, distribution, and political situations in various countries when making decisions.

Sales Ability—Using appropriate interpersonal styles and communication methods to gain acceptance of an idea, plan, activity, service, or product from prospects and customers.

B

BEHAVIORAL DIMENSIONS BY JOB CLUSTER

To help you better define the behavioral dimensions for the position you are seeking, this appendix shows the dimensions from Appendix A organized by clusters of jobs. Remember that the motivational and knowledge/skill dimensions are not shown. Also note that there is considerable variation in the dimensions among jobs in each cluster.

Dimension	Traditional Employee	Empowered Employee	Traditional Supervisor	Empowered Supervisor	Middle Manager	Executive	Sales	Engineer/ Scientist
Adaptability					x	x	x	
Building Trust				x	x	x		
Continuous Learning and Growth		x		x	x	x	x	x
Creativity/Innovation								x
Energy	x	x	x	x	x	x	x	x
Initiative	x	x	x	x	x	x	x	x
Integrity					x	x	x	
Stress Tolerance					x		x	x
Tenacity							x	x
Coaching		x		x				
Communication	x	x	x	x	x	x	x	x
Teamwork/Building Partnerships/Collaboration		x		x	x	x	x	x
Valuing Diversity	x	x		x	x	x		
Leadership and Influence			x	x				
Meeting Participation/ Leadership		x		x				x
Sharing Responsibility				x	x	x		
Decision Making		x	x	x	x	x	x	x
Decisiveness					x	x	x	x
Planning and Organizing		x	x	x	x	x	x	x
Customer Orientation		x		x	x	x	x	x
Global Perspective						x	x	
Sales Ability							x	

C

BIG FIVE BEHAVIORAL DIMENSIONS (WHEN IN DOUBT, ASSUME THAT THESE ARE IMPORTANT TO THE JOB YOU ARE SEEKING)

Continuous Learning and Growth—Assimilating and applying in a timely manner new job-related information that may vary in complexity; possessing intellectual agility needed to learn new concepts and tasks; showing eagerness and enthusiasm for learning new tasks and taking on additional responsibilities; taking the initiative in development activities; seeking and accepting feedback and coaching.

Teamwork/Building Partnerships/ Collaboration—Working collaboratively and cooperatively with others; building relationships; working effectively with team or work group or those outside the formal line of authority (e.g., associates, senior managers) to accomplish organizational goals; taking actions that respect the needs and contributions of others; contributing to and accepting the consensus; subordinating own objectives to the objectives of the organization or team.

Communication—Expressing thoughts, feelings, and ideas effectively in individual and group situations (including nonverbal communication); presenting ideas effectively when given time for preparation (including use of visual aids); clearly expressing ideas in memoranda, letters, or reports that have appropriate organization and structure and correct grammar, language, and terminology;

adjusting language to the characteristics and needs of the audience.

Decision Making—Identifying and understanding issues and problems; utilizing effective approaches for choosing a course of action or developing appropriate solutions; taking action that is consistent with available facts, constraints, and probable consequences.

Initiative—Asserting one's influence over events to achieve goals; self-starting rather than accepting passively; taking action to achieve goals beyond what is required; being proactive.

D

A NOTE ON CAREER PLANNING

Though we've discussed the concepts in this book in terms of how they can help you prepare for a job interview, they might also be useful to you in planning your career and professional development. Our approach to career planning—which looks at motivation first—presents for many people a fundamentally different way of looking at the future. Consider it a challenge or a call for continuous learning.

When making long-term career decisions, begin with your own dimension profile. You can use the preparation exercises in chapters 3, 4, and 5 to give yourself a complete picture of your dimensions.

Your long-term goal should be to find a job that will closely match this profile. Don't make the mistake of trying to find a job exactly like the one you lost when your organization downsized. It's possible that similar jobs are being eliminated in other organizations too because of changing technology or markets. Instead, begin with an analysis of your motivators and demotivators. It's most important to look for a job with the best motivational fit possible because these facets are unlikely to change within you or within the job you seek.

Acknowledgments

Thank you for your hard work in managing all the resources needed to create the graphics for this book.

Amy Plitt: We're so grateful to you for your work on our final edit. We really needed someone to see if our exercises made sense. We just hope you apply the skills you learned from the book in interviews for internal jobs only!

Bill Proudfoot: You helped us find the direction to finish what we'd started. Thank you for your work on this book and for your management of editorial work in general, which allowed Mary to focus her efforts on this project while still meeting everyone else's needs.

Holly White: Your willingness to pitch in and help us with our last-minute formatting changes ("No pressure, but this is for the CEO") was much appreciated. Thank you for struggling with our handwriting and for joining in our enthusiasm.

Thank you, also, to those who provided valuable early reviews and suggestions.

DDI Associates:

Tacy Byham Lehman
Mary Del Rossa
Jim Drummond
Eric Elder
Dick Gage
Jamie Hess
Bill Jackson
Merrideth Miller
Ruth Moskowitz
Pam Owens
Bob Rogers
Pat Smith

Clients and Colleagues:

InVenture Group, Inc.
Cybele Eidenschenk, Glamour Magazine
Maryanne Eisenreich, Carlow College
Nancy Gaffner and others at HAN Communications
Scott Helsel, BMG Entertainment
Steve Hokey, Copeland Corporation
Daniel Hurwitz, Witt-Thomas Productions
Tom Jorgensen, Tom Jorgensen Design
Leslie Killahan, International Paper
Steven Krauzer, University of Montana
Gene Rice, Sales Consultants International

Acknowledgments

Writing and producing *Landing the Job You Want* was truly a team effort. Many people contributed ideas, critiqued various drafts, and provided encouragement along the way. We deeply appreciate their interest, support, and involvement. DDI associates who deserve special recognition include:

Lynne Amatangelo: When many of us were winding down, you were just gearing up. Thank you for all of your work in coordinating the final production of this book.

David Biber: Your infinite patience, flexibility, and good humor did not go unnoticed. Thank you for the time and effort you put into the artistic design of this book. Most of all, thank you for coordinating all our last-minute changes, last-minute changes, and last-minute changes.

Jessica Bruckner: You blended inspiration with just the right amount of distraction. Your experiences and ideas have filled our pages. Thank you for the book party—it was actually the main goal all along.

Shawn Garry: Thanks for making sure we crossed all our t's and dotted all our i's. We spent so much time with this book and made so many changes, that by the time we passed it to you, we could barely see straight. Thanks for lending us your very keen eyes.

Gene Hunt: The model of empowering leadership, a manager who encouraged his assistant to pursue a project with the company's CEO. Thank you for giving Debra the time and tools to make this happen. Without you and your team, it would not have been possible.

Anne Maers: Your management of this project has been exemplary. Thank you for all your work in coordinating our reviews, distribution, and marketing.

Mary Matzen: Though we sometimes shuddered when you marched into our meetings armed with your trusty red pen, we all have come to admire your impeccable standards and your ability to work under the pressure of our occasionally unreasonable deadlines. Thank you for your management of the editing and proofreading of this book and for reminding us all of what was really important.

Helen Moretti: We're still amazed at the magic you worked with our calendars. The impossible you did immediately, while still managing to keep us on schedule and on task. Thank you for coordinating the many meetings and brainstorming sessions that made this project happen.

Karen Munch: You were the first to take on the challenge of designing a text format that would bring to life the many voices in this book.

About Development Dimensions International

At DDI we believe the workforce is the most critical factor in achieving organizational success. For more than 27 years, we've been helping organizations select and develop empowered, high-involvement workforces.

Since being founded in 1970, DDI has served more than 16,000 clients around the world, spanning a diverse range of industries and including more than 400 of the *Fortune* 500 corporations.

We are the only major human resource provider in the world to address and fully integrate the three areas essential to successful high involvement: organizational change consulting, assessment and selection systems, and training and development programs.

DDI's corporate headquarters and distribution facilities are located in Pittsburgh, Pennsylvania. It maintains 71 offices around the world, including regional training centers in Atlanta, Chicago, Dallas, Denver, Los Angeles, New York, and San Francisco, as well as operations in Argentina, Australia, Brazil, Canada, Chile, China, Finland, France, Germany, Hong Kong, Indonesia, Japan, Korea, Peru, the Philippines, South Africa, Spain, Switzerland, and the United Kingdom. DDI's programs are available in 19 languages.

For more information about the programs and services available from Development Dimensions International, call us between 7:30 a.m. and 5:30 p.m. EST at 1-800-933-4463 in the U.S. or 1-800-668-7971 in Canada.

Also, we'd love to hear about your reactions to *Landing the Job You Want*. Send your comments to William C. Byham, President/CEO, Development Dimensions International, World Headquarters—Pittsburgh, 1225 Washington Pike, Bridgeville, PA 15017-2838, or to one of the following e-mail addresses: Internet web site at info@ddiworld.com or the Microsoft® network at ddi@msn.com.

Visit Our Website to Send Your Profile

If you have completed the preparation exercises in this book, you can add your dimensional profile to DDI's database of job seekers. Visit our website at http://www.ddiworld.com and click on the "Land the Job" icon. You'll find a generic resume form, and lists of knowledge/skill and behavioral dimensions and facets of motivational fit. If you provide background information, ratings of your strengths in the dimensions, and the motivational facets important to you, we'll make this information available to clients looking for employees. This is a free service, and while we can't guarantee that you'll land a job, we offer you this opportunity to present what you've learned about yourself.

Similarly, some of the behavioral dimensions you possess or lack (for example, stress tolerance and tolerance for ambiguity) are difficult to change and should be your next consideration. Behavioral dimensions that you can develop (you be the judge) should be given less weight in your decision because you can always work on improving these areas.

When you focus on finding a job that matches your motivation and behaviors, you might find that there are mismatches in your knowledge/skill profile and the knowledge/skill dimensions required by the job. Thinking in the long term will enable you to plan for the development of the skills you'll need.

Adding Dimensions to Your Resume

Refining or developing your resume is an important part of the career-planning process. It's really a natural outgrowth of the work that you do in analyzing your dimensions. Because many companies are now using computers to scan resumes and match applicants to jobs, it is to your advantage to use the same language—dimensions or competencies—that human resource professionals use. As you list your job experience, consider using dimensions, rather than specific tasks, to describe your responsibilities. For example, an administrative job might be listed as follows:

1994-1996 **Widgets International,** Mudville, USA
Assistant to the President

Planning and Organizing
Managed appearances and speeches at conferences and conventions.

Written Communication
Authored speeches and correspondence.

Initiative
Administrative responsibility for office; made decisions in boss' absence.

Analysis and Problem Solving
Troubleshooting for travel arrangements, appearances, and meetings.

Other Books by William C. Byham and Others at DDI

Select the right people for your organization:

The Selection Solution: Solving the Mystery of Matching People to Jobs by William C. Byham with Steven M. Krauzer

Build an empowered organization:

The Service Leaders Club by William C. Byham with Jim Davis and Ray Crew

Zapp!® The Lightning of Empowerment by William C. Byham with Jeff Cox (also available on videocassette and audiocassette)

Zapp!® in Education by William C. Byham with Jeff Cox and Kathy Harper Shomo

Zapp!®: Empowerment in Health Care by William C. Byham with Jeff Cox and Greg Nelson

HeroZ™: Empower Yourself, Your Coworkers, Your Company by William C. Byham and Jeff Cox (also available on audiocassette)

Create and sustain high-performance work teams:

Empowered Teams: Creating Self-Directed Work Groups That Improve Quality, Productivity, and Participation by Richard S. Wellins, William C. Byham, and Jeanne M. Wilson

Inside Teams: How 20 World-Class Organizations Are Winning Through Teamwork by Richard S. Wellins, William C. Byham, and George Dixon

Leadership Trapeze: Strategies for Leadership in Team-Based Organizations by Jeanne M. Wilson, Jill George, and Richard S. Wellins, with William C. Byham

Succeeding With Teams: 101 Tips That Really Work by Richard S. Wellins, Dick Schaaf, and Kathy Harper Shomo

Team Leader's Survival Guide by Jeanne M. Wilson and Jill A. George

Team Member's Survival Guide by Jill A. George and Jeanne M. Wilson

Understand how Japanese companies operate outside Japan:

Shogun Management™: How North Americans Can Thrive in Japanese Companies by William C. Byham with George Dixon

About the Authors

William C. Byham, Ph.D., has been called "the world's foremost authority on hiring."*

He has written numerous books and articles on methods of employee assessment and selection, including his 1996 book, *The Selection Solution: Solving the Mystery of Matching People to Jobs.*

In 1972 Dr. Byham developed Targeted Selection, the most widely used interviewer training program in the world. The Targeted Selection program teaches interviewers how to make accurate hiring decisions by evaluating a person's past job behaviors (acquired through interviews) and current behaviors (observed in simulations) against the dimensions (competencies) required for success in an open position.

In addition to Dr. Byham's work to improve organizations' selection and promotion decisions, he has researched and written extensively on identifying "job dimensions" that relate to job success in both the present and the future. This fits well with another of Dr. Byham's interests, how to develop an empowered workforce.
Dr. Byham is the author of the international best-selling books, *Zapp!® The Lightning of Empowerment* and *HeroZ™: Empower Yourself, Your Coworkers, Your Company.*

Dr. Byham is president and CEO of Development Dimensions International, a leading provider of programs and services designed to help organizations identify, hire, and develop their employees.

Debra Pickett began her career with Development Dimensions International as a member of its New York-based sales team. She currently serves as a communications specialist at DDI's corporate headquarters, where she authors proposals for major consulting projects and articles and speeches for senior executives.

Having developed the story line for *Landing the Job You Want,* Ms. Pickett is presently at work on several other projects, including a novel based on her own job search and early career.

*Carbonara, P. (1996, August/September). Hire for attitude, train for skill. *Fast Company Magazine.* 73-81